JESUS

*The God Who Knows
Your Name*

STUDY GUIDE | SIX SESSIONS

MAX LUCADO

THOMAS NELSON
Since 1798

Jesus Study Guide
© 2020 by Max Lucado

Published in Nashville, Tennessee, by Thomas Nelson. Thomas Nelson is a registered trademark of HarperCollins Christian Publishing, Inc.

Published in association with Anvil II Management, Inc.

All Scripture quotations, unless otherwise noted, are taken from the Holy Bible, New International Version®. NIV ®. Copyright 1973, 1978, 1994, 2011 by Biblica, Inc.®. Used by permission. All rights reserved worldwide.

Scripture quotations marked AMP are taken from The Amplified Bible. Copyright © 2015 by The Lockman Foundation, La Habra, CA 90631. All rights reserved.

Scripture quotations marked ESV are taken from The Holy Bible, English Standard Version®. Copyright © 2001 by Crossway, a publishing ministry of Good News Publishers.

Scripture quotations marked MSG are taken from The Message. Copyright © 1993, 1994, 1995, 1996, 2000, 2001, 2002. Used by permission of NavPress Publishing Group.

Scripture quotations marked NCV are taken from the New Century Version®. Copyright © 2005 by Thomas Nelson. Used by permission. All rights reserved.

Scripture quotations marked NKJV taken from the New King James Version®. Copyright © 1982 by Thomas Nelson. Used by permission. All rights reserved.

Scripture quotations marked NLT are taken from the Holy Bible, New Living Translation, copyright © 1996, 2004, 2015 by Tyndale House Foundation. Used by permission of Tyndale House Publishers, Inc., Carol Stream, Illinois 60188. All rights reserved.

Scripture quotations marked NRSV are taken from New Revised Standard Version Bible, copyright © 1989 the Division of Christian Education of the National Council of the Churches of Christ in the United States of America. Used by permission. All rights reserved.

Thomas Nelson titles may be purchased in bulk for educational, business, fundraising, or sales promotional use. For information, e-mail SpecialMarkets@ThomasNelson.com.

ISBN 978-0-310-10583-1 (softcover)
ISBN 978-0-310-10584-8 (ebook)

First Printing November 2019 / Printed in the United States of America

Contents

A Word from Max Lucado

Are you open to the idea of a Father, a heavenly Father, who knows you? A soon-to-be home that awaits you? Would you consider this life-changing idea: the all-mighty and all-knowing God has set his affection on you? Every detail about you he knows. Your interests, your hang-ups. Your fears and failures. He knows you.

About his children God says, "The LORD searches every heart and understands every desire and every thought" (1 Chronicles 28:9).

He regards you as "the apple of his eye" (Zechariah 2:8).

He can "empathize with our weaknesses" (Hebrews 4:15).

"When my spirit was overwhelmed within me," King David wrote, "You knew my path" (Psalm 142:3 NKJV).

"He knows the way that I take," declared Job (Job 23:10).

Do you know this God who knows you? He knows your name. And he can't wait to get you home. This is the ever-recurring, soul-lifting message of heaven.

"The LORD delights in you" (Isaiah 62:4 NKJV).

"Fear not, for I have redeemed you; I have called you by your name; You are Mine" (Isaiah 43:1 NKJV).

"I have written your name on the palms of my hands" (Isaiah 49:16 NLT).

"The Lord takes pleasure in those who fear Him, in those who hope in His mercy" (Psalm 147:11 NKJV).

"The LORD directs the steps of the godly. He delights in every detail of their lives. Though they stumble, they will never fall, for the LORD holds them by the hand" (Psalm 37:23–24 NLT).

Do such words surprise you? Where did we get this idea of a God who does not care, who is not near? We certainly didn't get it from Jesus.

Jesus Christ is the perfect picture of God. Want to know how God feels about the sick? Look at Jesus. What angers God? Look at Jesus. Does God ever give up on people? Does he stand up for people? Find the answer in Jesus. "The Son is the radiance and only expression of the glory of [our awesome] God . . . and the exact representation and perfect imprint of His [Father's] essence" (Hebrews 1:3 AMP).

The purpose of this study is simple: *to get to know Jesus.* You will study who Jesus was while he walked on this earth and what that means for your life today. In doing this, you will get to know God, his purpose for you, and his love for you like you never have before.

The Son is the radiance of his Father. Are you ready to meet him?

How to Use This Guide

The *Jesus Video Study* is designed to be experienced in a group setting such as a Bible study, Sunday school class, or any small group gathering. Each session begins with a brief opening reflection and questions to get you and your group thinking about the topic. You will then watch a video with Max Lucado and jump into some directed small-group discussion. You will close each session with a time of prayer as a group. Each person should have his or her own study guide, which includes video teaching notes, group discussion questions, and between-sessions personal studies to help you apply the material to your life during the week.

To get the most out of your group experience, keep the following points in mind. First, the real growth in this study will happen during your small-group time. This is where you will process the content of the teaching, ask questions, and learn from others as you hear what God is doing in their lives. For this reason, it is important for you to be fully committed to the group and attend each session so you can build trust and rapport with the other members. If you choose to only "go through the motions," or if you refrain from participating, there is a lesser chance you will find what you're looking for during this study.

Second, remember the goal of your small group is to serve as a place where people can share, learn about God, and build intimacy and friendship. For this reason, seek to make your group a "safe place." This means being honest about your thoughts and feelings and listening carefully to everyone else's opinion. (**Note:** *If you are a group leader, there are additional instructions and resources in the back of the book for leading a productive discussion group.*)

Third, resist the temptation to "fix" a problem someone might be having or to correct his or her theology, as that's not the purpose of your small-group time. Also, keep everything your group shares confidential. This will foster a rewarding sense of community in your group and create a place where people can heal, be challenged, and grow spiritually.

Following your group time, maximize the impact of the course with the additional between-session studies. For each session, you may wish to complete the personal study all in one sitting or spread it out over a few days (for example, working on it a half hour a day on three different days that week). Note that if you are unable to finish (or even start!) your between-sessions personal study, you should still attend the group study video session. You are still wanted and welcome at the group even if you don't have your "homework" done.

Keep in mind the videos, discussions, and activities are simply meant to kick-start your imagination so you are not only open to what God wants you to hear but also how to apply it to your life. So be watching for what God is saying to you as you and your group go through this study on the birth, ministry, healings, teachings, sacrifice, and resurrection of Jesus. Remember that he is "the God who sees" (Genesis 16:13) . . . and that he knows your name.

GOD WITH US

In the beginning was the Word, and the Word was with God, and the Word was God. He was with God in the beginning. Through him all things were made; without him nothing was made that has been made. In him was life, and that life was the light of all mankind. The light shines in the darkness, and the darkness has not overcome it. . . . The Word became flesh and made his dwelling among us. We have seen his glory, the glory of the one and only Son, who came from the Father, full of grace and truth.

JOHN 1:1–5, 14

OPENING REFLECTION

When you were a child, what did you think clouds were made of? Cotton? Pillows? Something springy and soft? When you're young, it's hard to wrap your mind around the idea of air, ice particles, and liquid coming together to form a mass that—were you to touch it—would feel like nothing. To understand the concept of a cloud, it helps to initially put substance around it.

The concept of God can be equally difficult to wrap our minds around, even as adults. He is everywhere. He is outside of time. He is on the earth, but he is outside the earth. What does he look like, exactly? Where does he dwell, exactly? Is he up or down? East or west?

Jesus came to earth as the first tangible presence of God. Paul writes, "Christ himself was like God in everything. . . . He was born as a man and became like a servant" (Philippians 2:6-7 NCV). Jesus was a man, but he was also God. His role is summed up well in the Hebrew word *Immanuel*, which means "God with us."

God sent Jesus so we would know what he was like and know that he understands us. Jesus was fully human, so he experienced the daily life of a human of his time. He experienced our physical limitations and the emotional pain, grief, and happiness we've all experienced on this earth. God sent Jesus to tell us he knows what it is like to be a human in this world.

Because of Jesus, God is no longer a confusing, ethereal, unformed being located somewhere in the sky. Instead, God is right here. Near us and with us. *Immanuel*. In this session, you will take a deeper look into the biblical story of how Jesus arrived on earth, why he came the way that he did, and what all of this can teach you about God.

TALK ABOUT IT

If you or any of your group members are just getting to know one another, take a few minutes to introduce yourselves. Then, to kick things off for this first session, discuss one of the following questions:

- What comes to your mind when you try to picture what God is like?

  — or —

- How do you respond to the fact that Jesus experienced everything you experience here on earth—including the range of human emotions?

VIDEO TEACHING NOTES

Play the video segment for session one. As you watch, use the following outline to record any thoughts or concepts that stand out to you.

NOTES

Jesus was *fully divine*. All-knowing. All-present. All-powerful. Yet the Bible makes it clear he was also *fully human*. "He was born as a man and became like a servant" (Philippians 2:7 NCV).

There is something about keeping Jesus divine that keeps him distant, packaged, and predictable. But let's remember that the people who saw him first . . . saw him first as a person.

God had asked Joseph to go out on a limb. he was left with a hard choice: follow his will or the Lord's. In the end, he knew there was only one option. For the only thing worse to Joseph than a venture into the unknown was denying his Master.

Gabriel had to wonder: *God will become a baby?* The heavens themselves could not contain him. To imagine some mother burping God on her shoulder . . . well, that was beyond what even an angel could imagine.

The hometown of God would be a single-camel map dot on the edge of boredom. His earthly mother, Mary, was a Jewish peasant who had barely outgrown her acne. Joseph was a student of the Bible . . . but at the end of the day just a carpenter.

Fast-forward nine months. Mary and Joseph have made their way to the village of Bethlehem. Jesus will be born in a stable on the outskirts of town. It stinks, like all stables do. The stench of urine, dung, and sheep hangs in the air.

Were it not for the shepherds, there would have been no reception. And were it not for a group of star-gazers, there would have been no gifts. God has led them to Jerusalem with a star. But he leads them to Jesus with Scripture. They are the first Christian worshipers.

At times, that limb on which Joseph sat bounced furiously in the wind. But Joseph just shut his eyes and held on. And you can be sure of one thing: he never regretted it.

God wants us to know he *gets* us. Are your looks run-of-the-mill and your ways simple? So were Jesus'. Do you struggle financially? Jesus knows how you feel. Are you on the lower rungs of the social ladder? So was he. Ever feel betrayed? Christ can certainly relate. Our God gets us.

GROUP DISCUSSION

Take a few minutes with your group members to discuss what you just watched and explore these concepts in Scripture.

1. What words, thoughts, or images come to mind when you hear the name *Jesus*? Where do these come from? The Bible, your upbringing, a sermon you heard? Explain.

2. Read Philippians 2:6–7. Jesus was fully divine, but he was also all-human. Do you tend to think of Jesus as more divine, more human, or both? Why?

3. Read the angel's announcement to Joseph in Matthew 1:20–25. If you were Joseph, how do you think you would have reacted to this news? How did Joseph actually respond to the angel's message? What does this tell you about Joseph's character?

4. Now read the angel's announcement to Mary in Luke 1:28–38. If you were Mary, how would you have reacted

to this news? How *did* Mary respond to the angel's message? What does this tell you about Mary's character?

5. Have you ever sensed God asking you to step out on a limb, much like he asked Joseph and Mary to do? If so, what was your initial response to the calling? What do you now see was the purpose for your—or someone else's—life for going out on a limb like this?

6. Read Luke 2:8–18 and Matthew 2:1–12. What role did the shepherds and the magi (or wise men) play in Jesus' birth? What role did King Herod play in these events?

7. What is something new or surprising you learned about the birth of Christ in this session? What do you think is the most interesting or compelling part of this narrative?

8. As you reflect on everything discussed today, why did God send Jesus to earth in the way that he did—as a baby, born to a normal family, and placed in a normal town?

CLOSING ACTIVITY

Briefly review the outline for the video teaching and any notes you took. In the space below, write down what it means to you that God chose to become flesh and live among us. How does that help you to know that God understands everything that you are going through? How does it change your perspective of him? What comfort does that provide to you? If you feel comfortable, share what you have written with the rest of the group.

Closing Prayer

One of the most important things you and your group members can do as a community is to pray for one another. This is not simply a closing prayer to end the group time but also a time to share prayer requests and review what God has done in your lives. So, in the space below, record any prayer requests from your group members, and then commit to praying for those requests throughout the week. Also record any praise reports that people have to share.

NAME   PRAYER REQUEST / PRAISE REPORT

SESSION ONE

BETWEEN-SESSIONS
PERSONAL STUDY

Reflect on the material you have covered during your group time by engaging in the following between-sessions activities. This week, you will take a closer look at the story of Jesus' birth as told in the Gospels. Each personal study consists of three days of reflection activities to help you implement what you learned in the group time. The time you invest will be well spent, so grab a Bible (or open your Bible app), a cup of coffee or tea, a pen, and allow God to reveal his truth to you by studying his Word. At your next meeting, share any key points or insights that stood out to you as you spent this time with the Lord.

PREPARE THE WAY FOR HIM

The story of Jesus' birth in the Gospel of Luke actually begins with the birth of Jesus' cousin, John the Baptist. Just as with Jesus, an angel prophesied about the birth of John to his father, a priest named Zechariah. Read the following prophecy found in Luke 1:13–17:

¹³ *"Do not be afraid, Zechariah; your prayer has been heard. Your wife Elizabeth will bear you a son, and you are to call him John. ¹⁴ He will be a joy and delight to you, and many will rejoice because of his birth, ¹⁵ for he will be great in the sight of the Lord.... ¹⁶ He will bring back many of the people of Israel to the Lord their God. ¹⁷ And he will go on before the Lord, in the spirit and power of Elijah, to turn the hearts of the parents to their children and the disobedient to the wisdom of the righteous—to make ready a people prepared for the Lord."*

1. What did the angel say that John would bring? What would be his primary purpose as it related to the coming of the Messiah?

2. After John was born, "Zechariah was filled with the Holy Spirit and prophesied" (Luke 1:67). Read the following portion of that prophecy in Luke 1:76–78:

   ⁷⁶ *"And you, my child, will be called a prophet of the Most High; for you will go on before the Lord to prepare the way for him, ⁷⁷ to give his people the knowledge of salvation through the forgiveness of their sins, ⁷⁸ because of the tender mercy of our God."*

3. What would John do for the Lord? What knowledge would he give to the people? Why would the people receive forgiveness for their sins?

4. Jesus' birth had been foretold long before the birth of John the Baptist. God had been preparing the world for Jesus' arrival for hundreds of years, as these prophecies relate:

Therefore the LORD *himself will give you a sign: The virgin will conceive and give birth to a son, and will call him Immanuel* (Isaiah 7:14).

A shoot will come up from the stump of Jesse; from his roots a Branch will bear fruit. The Spirit of the LORD *will rest on him* (Isaiah 11:1–2).

A voice of one calling: "In the wilderness prepare the way for the Lord; make straight in the desert a highway for our God. Every valley shall be raised up, every mountain and hill made low; the rough ground shall become level, the rugged places a plain. And the glory of the LORD *will be revealed, and all people will see it together. For the mouth of the* LORD *has spoken"* (Isaiah 40:3–5).

According to these prophecies, how would Jesus be born? What would he be like? Why would he choose to come into this world?

5. Why do you think God chose to announce the coming of his Son—the Messiah—to his people for so many years?

6. John the Baptist's purpose was to prepare the way for Jesus by readying the Israelites for his arrival. Why do you think it was important for him to do this?

7. Consider some things that God has prepared you for ahead of time. Why do you think God chose to prepare you in this manner?

8. How do you react when you read that God chose to send his Son into the world to experience *everything* that you experience? How did this make you feel *known* by God?

Closing reflection: Pick one passage from today's study and read over it a few times to yourself or out loud. Ask God to reveal any new insights he might have for you from that passage. End your time in prayer, thanking God for the gift of his Word and for choosing to send his only Son into the world. Also ask that God would prepare your heart and your mind for the day ahead.

MARY AND JOSEPH AND SHEPHERDS . . . OH MAGI!

Jesus' birth included a cast of characters, all of whom played an important role in the story. Spend some time today studying their different responses to Christ's birth and early years.

MARY

Mary traveled to a town in the hill country of Judea to see her cousin Elizabeth shortly after the angel announced she would give birth to the Messiah. Elizabeth greeted Mary and quickly recognized (through the power of the Holy Spirit) that Mary was pregnant with the Messiah. Soon after, Mary broke into song:

> [46] *"My soul glorifies the Lord*
>> [47] *and my spirit rejoices in God my Savior,*
> [48] *for he has been mindful*
>> *of the humble state of his servant.*
> *From now on all generations will call me blessed,*
>> [49] *for the Mighty One has done great things for me—*
>> *holy is his name"* (Luke 1:46–49).

1. What is the overall tone of Mary's song? How does Mary describe God in these verses?

2. How would you say Mary responded to the prophecy of Christ's birth?

JOSEPH

Joseph was planning to quietly divorce Mary after he found out she was pregnant. But then an angel came to him and told him about God's plan:

> [20] *But after he had considered this, an angel of the Lord appeared to him in a dream and said, "Joseph son of David,*

*do not be afraid to take Mary home as your wife, because
what is conceived in her is from the Holy Spirit.* [21] *She will
give birth to a son, and you are to give him the name Jesus,
because he will save his people from their sins." . . .*

[24] *When Joseph woke up, he did what the angel of the
Lord had commanded him and took Mary home as his wife.*
[25] *But he did not consummate their marriage until she gave
birth to a son. And he gave him the name Jesus* (Matthew
1:20–21, 24–25).

3. What specific instructions did the angel give to Joseph?

4. How did Joseph respond to the message from the angel?

THE SHEPHERDS

In a field near the town of Bethlehem, an angel of the Lord
appeared to a group of shepherds to announce the coming of
the Messiah. The glory of the Lord shone around the shepherds, and they were terrified. But the angel said to them,
"Do not be afraid. I bring you good news that will cause great
joy for all the people. Today in the town of David a Savior has
been born to you; he is the Messiah, the Lord" (Luke 2:10–11).
After the angel had said this:

13 *Suddenly a great company of the heavenly host appeared with the angel, praising God and saying,*

14 *"Glory to God in the highest heaven, and on earth peace to those on whom his favor rests."*

15 *When the angels had left them and gone into heaven, the shepherds said to one another, "Let's go to Bethlehem and see this thing that has happened, which the Lord has told us about."*

16 *So they hurried off and found Mary and Joseph, and the baby, who was lying in the manger.* 17 *When they had seen him, they spread the word concerning what had been told them about this child,* 18 *and all who heard it were amazed at what the shepherds said to them* (Luke 2:13–18).

5. What did the shepherds say to each other after the appearance of the heavenly host?

6. What actions did they take next? How did others respond to what the shepherds said?

THE MAGI AND KING HEROD

King Herod, the ruler of Judea, had a completely different response when he learned from the Magi that a "king of the

Jews" had been born. Herod saw the birth of Jesus as a threat to his own rule and plotted to kill the newborn . . . though he tried to keep this from the Magi so they would find the child for him. But God had other plans:

> [1] *Magi from the east came to Jerusalem* [2] *and asked, "Where is the one who has been born king of the Jews? We saw his star when it rose and have come to worship him."*
>
> [3] *When King Herod heard this he was disturbed, and all Jerusalem with him. . . .*
>
> [7] *Then Herod called the Magi secretly and found out from them the exact time the star had appeared.* [8] *He sent them to Bethlehem and said, "Go and search carefully for the child. As soon as you find him, report to me, so that I too may go and worship him." . . .*
>
> [11] *On coming to the house, they saw the child with his mother Mary, and they bowed down and worshiped him. Then they opened their treasures and presented him with gifts of gold, frankincense and myrrh.* [12] *And having been warned in a dream not to go back to Herod, they returned to their country by another route* (Matthew 2:1–3, 7–8, 11–12).

7. How did Herod feel when he heard about the birth of Jesus? How do you think this affected the entire city of Jerusalem as well?

8. How did the Magi respond when they finally came to the home of Jesus?

YOUR RESPONSE

Each person in the story responded to Jesus' birth differently. Mary worshiped God. Joseph was obedient. The shepherds spread the news. King Herod felt threatened. The Magi offered gifts and chose to follow God above Herod's orders. We have all likely had similar responses to Jesus and the gospel. Like Mary, sometimes we are moved to worship. Like Joseph, sometimes we are simply obedient with our actions. Like the shepherds, sometimes we want to spread the good news. Like King Herod, we may feel disturbed by the truth. And like the magi, sometimes we decide to give of ourselves and honor Jesus above all earthly authority. Use the space below to write about a time you responded to the gospel like the characters you studied today:

Mary:

Joseph:

The shepherds:

King Herod:

The Magi:

Closing reflection: Determine where you are today in your posture toward the gospel. Which character do you resonate with most? Ask God to come alongside you, wherever you are, and be honest with him. If you need faith, ask him for it. If you feel like worshiping, worship him. If you want to give him the gift of your presence, time, or service to others, ask how you can do these things. Know that God is not waiting for you to be in a "good" place in your faith. He wants to talk to you today and can work through you *now* . . . no matter where you are.

WHY DID GOD DO IT?

It is important to know *how* Jesus came into this world. However, unless you understand *why* he came into this world, the story of Jesus' incarnation is just that—a story. At the end of this week's teaching, you considered the question, "Why did God do it?" In other words, why did God send his Son to live on the earth as fully human and fully God? This is what you will look at today.

1. In your own words, how would you answer the question as to *why* God chose to send his Son to the earth in the manner that he did?

2. How would you describe who Jesus is to you? Where did this image or idea come from?

3. The author of Hebrews provides the following insights into the coming of Jesus:

   Now that we know what we have—Jesus, this great High Priest with ready access to God—let's not let it slip through our fingers. We don't have a priest who is out of touch with our reality. He's been through weakness and testing, experienced it all—all but the sin. So let's walk right up to him and get what he is so ready to give. Take the mercy, accept the help (Hebrews 4:14–16 MSG).

   List all of the words used to describe Jesus. What has Jesus been through?

4. Have you ever shared something difficult with a friend and he or she responded, "Me too"? How did that experience make you feel? Why?

5. Do you believe that no matter what you are going through or have been through, Jesus could say in response, "Me too"? Why or why not?

6. What is something you would like to share with Jesus today, knowing that he completely understands what you are facing? How does it feel to bring this to him?

Closing reflection: Use your prayer time to share with Jesus what you wrote in response to this last question. Share it as you would with a friend whom you know would say, "Me too." Then, sit and be still. Just listen. Did you hear Jesus speak to this pain, confession, or hurt in any way? If so, what did he say? If you didn't hear anything, that is okay. Just observe how this experience of sharing something intimate with Christ made you feel.

FURTHER REFLECTION

Reflect on what you studied this week: the birth of Jesus, the reactions of the people to his coming, and how you can know that God *gets* you. Journal your thoughts on these topics or write them as a prayer to God, whether you need to ask him questions about what you learned, thank him for what you learned, or ask him what to do next now that you have a better understanding. Also write down any observations or questions that you want to bring to your next group time.

SESSION TWO

FRIEND OF SINNERS

All the people saw this and began to mutter,
"He has gone to be the guest of a sinner." But Zacchaeus stood
up and said to the Lord, "Look, Lord! Here and now I give
half of my possessions to the poor, and if I have cheated
anybody out of anything, I will pay back four times the
amount." Jesus said to him, "Today salvation has come to this
house, because this man, too, is a son of Abraham. For the
Son of Man came to seek and to save the lost."

LUKE 19:7–10

OPENING REFLECTION

We live in a comparison-obsessed culture. In recent years, this need to size ourselves up to others has been intensified by social media. Now, we can compare ourselves to anyone at any time. Friends, family, celebrities—there is no shortage of opportunities for us to observe the photographed lives of others and feel inferior.

It's easy to read about the life of Jesus and default to this comparison mode. *A perfect human? Who never sinned? Who gave his life selflessly for others? How can he relate to me?* But the story of Jesus is not recorded in the Gospels for us to compare our lives to his—for the reality is we will *never* be able to measure up. Rather, "God made him who had *no sin* to be sin for us, so that in him we might become the righteousness of God" (2 Corinthians 5:21).

Yet the fact remains that Jesus *did* face all of the temptations that we face. In fact, he endured forty days of temptations from the enemy at the start of his ministry. Yet through it all, he remained faithful to his calling. He did not waiver. Not even once. The temptations, the loneliness, the despair—Jesus experienced it all. And he came out the other side.

This tells us that Jesus *can* relate to us. Furthermore, because he can relate, he does not fear our sin or cringe at our past. Nor does he refuse to fellowship with us or give us assignments because we are not as perfect as him. We realize this is true when we look at his cast of disciples—a group of fishermen and tax collectors and sinners who fumbled every step of the way during their time with him. Yet Jesus *chose them* to follow him.

As you study Jesus' life, pay close attention to the deeply human experiences he had. Let them draw you closer to him. Don't let comparison steal the joy of following Jesus. For the truth is that sin, faults, flaws, and all, he offers you the same invitation he offered Peter and Levi and the others: "Follow me and be my disciple" (Matthew 9:9 NLT).

TALK ABOUT IT

If you or any of your group members are just meeting for the first time, take a few minutes to introduce yourselves and share any insights that you have from last week's personal study. Then, to get things started for this group time, discuss one of the following questions:

- How do you picture Jesus interacting with the people of his day?

— *or* —

- Why is it significant that Jesus faced every temptation we face but did not sin?

VIDEO TEACHING NOTES

Play the video segment for session two. As you watch, use the following outline to record any thoughts or concepts that stand out to you.

NOTES

It must have been difficult for Jesus to leave Nazareth. Life had been peaceful there. And safe. But he knew it was time to leave. It was time to walk out of his earthly father's shop . . . and into the mission his heavenly Father had set before him.

From the beginning, Jesus identifies with the people's plight. With *our* plight. We owe God perfect obedience to every command. The problem is we can't deliver. But Christ *can*. His plunge into the Jordan is a picture of his plunge into our sin.

The Second Adam had come to succeed where the first Adam failed. Adam was challenged to remain sinless in a sinless world. Christ is challenged to remain sinless in a sin-ridden world. Jesus doesn't bite the bait. He never wavers.

This village of Capernaum becomes the base of operations for Jesus' ministry. The choice should surprise us. Capernaum is not a hub of academic learning, not the residence of scholars, nor of any political or military importance.

Peter meets Jesus after fishing all night. No matter what they tried, the sea had offered nothing. So he was in no mood to hear a well-rested carpenter-turned-rabbi say, "Put out into deep water, and let down the nets for a catch" (Luke 5:4).

Peter lifts his eyes off the catch and onto the face of Christ. At that moment, he sees Jesus—Jesus the *Lord*. He falls face-first among the fish. Their stink doesn't bother him. It is his stink that he's worried about.

Peter viewed himself as sinful. *Everyone* viewed Levi as a man in sin. Everybody kept their distance from him. Everyone except Christ. He sees potential in Levi. Levi sees redemption in Jesus. So Levi takes up Jesus' offer to follow him.

Matthew was a human . . . with very human failings. Just like you and me. This is why Jesus' words to Matthew should resonate so strongly with us: "Follow me" (Luke 5:27). Wherever you are, whatever you've done, you can still come to Christ.

GROUP DISCUSSION

Take a few minutes with your group members to discuss what you just watched and explore these concepts in Scripture.

1. Think about people who represent "Levi" in your world. What is the problem with looking down on them or judging them because of their past?

2. Read Matthew 3:13–15. Why did Jesus choose to be baptized by John?

3. In what ways is Jesus the "Second Adam"? What was similar between Adam's experience with temptation and Jesus' experience? What was different?

4. Read Luke 4:1–13. What was Satan's strategy when tempting Jesus? What was Jesus' strategy in responding to each of Satan's attacks?

5. Read Luke 4:28–30. Jesus returned to Nazareth and preached from the book of Isaiah. How did the people of Nazareth respond? Why do you think they responded this way? How do you think Jesus felt after the people in his hometown rejected him?

6. Read Luke 5:1–10. What did Peter recognize about himself in the presence of Jesus? What was your reaction to Jesus when you first met him?

7. What was the people's view of Levi? What caused the Pharisees to complain that Jesus was eating and drinking with "tax collectors and sinners" (Luke 5:30 NCV)?

8. How did Jesus see the potential in people like Peter and Levi? What does this tell you about writing someone off as "too far gone"?

CLOSING ACTIVITY

Briefly review the outline for the video teaching and any notes you took. In the space below, write down what it means that Jesus chose to associate with "sinners" like Peter and Levi. What does this say about the people he uses? How do you think God views you in light of these stories? If you feel comfortable, share what you have written with the the group.

CLOSING PRAYER

End your time in prayer, thanking God for sending Jesus to experience life as we know it, for giving us an example of perfection in Christ, and for forgiving our sins when we fall short of the mark. Pray that as you go forward this week, your relationship with Christ will deepen so you can hear him better, feel his love for you more deeply, and see his love for others more clearly. As in the previous session, record any prayer requests or praise reports from your group members, and commit to praying for them throughout the week.

NAME   PRAYER REQUEST / PRAISE REPORT

SESSION TWO

BETWEEN-SESSIONS
PERSONAL STUDY

Reflect on the material you have covered during your group time by engaging in the following between-sessions activities. This week, you will return to some of the locations discussed in the video and during your group time: the Garden of Eden, the wilderness where Jesus was tempted, and Jesus' hometown of Nazareth. Each personal study consists of three days of reflection activities to help you implement what you learned in the group time. The time you invest will be well spent, so let God use it to draw you closer to him. At your next meeting, share any key points or insights that stood out to you as you spent this time with the Lord.

THE GARDEN OF EDEN

In the teaching for this week, you looked at some of the comparisons between Jesus' temptation in the wilderness and Adam's temptation in the Garden of Eden. When God first created Adam and placed him in the garden, he said, "You are free to eat from any tree in the garden; but you must not eat from the tree of the knowledge of good and evil, for when you eat from it you will certainly die." Unfortunately, Adam and Eve did not follow this instruction:

> ¹ *Now the serpent was more crafty than any of the wild animals the* LORD *God had made. He said to the woman, "Did God really say, 'You must not eat from any tree in the garden'?"*
>
> ² *The woman said to the serpent, "We may eat fruit from the trees in the garden,* ³ *but God did say, 'You must not eat fruit from the tree that is in the middle of the garden, and you must not touch it, or you will die.'"*
>
> ⁴ *"You will not certainly die," the serpent said to the woman.* ⁵ *"For God knows that when you eat from it your eyes will be opened, and you will be like God, knowing good and evil."*
>
> ⁶ *When the woman saw that the fruit of the tree was good for food and pleasing to the eye, and also desirable for gaining wisdom, she took some and ate it. She also gave some to her husband, who was with her, and he ate it.* ⁷ *Then the eyes of both of them were opened, and they realized they were naked; so they sewed fig leaves together and made coverings for themselves.*
>
> ⁸ *Then the man and his wife heard the sound of the* LORD *God as he was walking in the garden in the cool of the day, and they hid from the* LORD *God among the trees of the garden.* ⁹ *But the* LORD *God called to the man, "Where are you?"*
>
> ¹⁰ *He answered, "I heard you in the garden, and I was afraid because I was naked; so I hid."*
>
> ¹¹ *And he said, "Who told you that you were naked? Have you eaten from the tree that I commanded you not to eat from?"*

[12] The man said, "The woman you put here with me— she gave me some fruit from the tree, and I ate it" (Genesis 3:1–12).

1. How did Satan challenge what God had said to Adam and Eve? What temptation did he then use to compel them to disobey God (see verses 1–5)?

2. What immediately happened to Adam and Eve after they sinned (see verse 7)?

3. How did God respond to their sin (see verses 8–9)?

4. How did Adam react when God asked if he had disobeyed his command (see verse 12)?

5. Adam and Eve's sin resulted in severe consequences that affect us even today:

[16] To the woman [God] said,

"I will make your pains in childbearing very severe;
*   with painful labor you will give birth to children.*

Your desire will be for your husband,
and he will rule over you."

¹⁷ *To Adam he said, "Because you listened to your wife*
and ate fruit from the tree about which I commanded you,
'You must not eat from it,'

"Cursed is the ground because of you;
through painful toil you will eat food from it
all the days of your life.
¹⁸ *It will produce thorns and thistles for you,*
and you will eat the plants of the field.
¹⁹ *By the sweat of your brow*
you will eat your food
until you return to the ground,
since from it you were taken;
for dust you are
and to dust you will return. . . ."

²³ *So the* LORD *God banished him from the Garden of*
Eden to work the ground from which he had been taken
(Genesis 3:16–19, 23).

What were the consequences of Eve's sin? What were
the consequences of Adam's sin?

6. Spend some time reflecting on the Fall and what it has meant for your life. Daily, how aware are you of your sin? Do you think about it often, sometimes, or hardly ever?

7. When have you especially felt the consequence for a sin you committed? How did you respond when you felt that conviction?

8. God went looking for Adam and Eve after they had sinned and called out their names. How do you think God responds to you when you sin? What do you think his thoughts are toward you when you make a mistake and fall into sin?

Closing reflection: Adam and Eve's sin was not the end of the story. It did not doom them . . . or us. God remained gracious and forgiving. End your time today by contemplating Psalm 36:5–9 below. You can simply read the passage to yourself, read it aloud, transcribe it in a journal, or even pray through it as you remember the lovingkindness of God your father.

THE WILDERNESS

As you saw in yesterday's study, Adam was tested in a garden, on a full stomach, and challenged to remain sinless in a sinless world. However, when Jesus began his ministry, he was tested in a stark wasteland, on an empty stomach, and challenged to remain sinless in a sin-ridden world. Luke writes the following in his Gospel about Jesus' forty days of temptation in the wilderness:

> [1] *Jesus, full of the Holy Spirit, left the Jordan and was led by the Spirit into the wilderness,* [2] *where for forty days he was tempted by the devil. He ate nothing during those days, and at the end of them he was hungry.*
>
> [3] *The devil said to him, "If you are the Son of God, tell this stone to become bread."*
>
> [4] *Jesus answered, "It is written: 'Man shall not live on bread alone.'"*
>
> [5] *The devil led him up to a high place and showed him in an instant all the kingdoms of the world.* [6] *And he said to him, "I will give you all their authority and splendor; it has been given to me, and I can give it to anyone I want to.* [7] *If you worship me, it will all be yours."*
>
> [8] *Jesus answered, "It is written: 'Worship the Lord your God and serve him only.'"*
>
> [9] *The devil led him to Jerusalem and had him stand on the highest point of the temple. "If you are the Son of God," he said, "throw yourself down from here.* [10] *For it is written:*
>
> > *"'He will command his angels concerning you*
> > *to guard you carefully;*

> [11] *they will lift you up in their hands,*
>   *so that you will not strike your foot against a stone.'"*

> [12] *Jesus answered, "It is said: 'Do not put the Lord your*
> *God to the test.'"*
> [13] *When the devil had finished all this tempting, he left*
> *him until an opportune time* (Luke 4:1–13).

1. What prompted Jesus to go into the wilderness (see verses 1–2)? Why do you think he was led to go there?

2. Jesus' temptation lasted a full *forty* days. Have you ever felt tempted or suffered from something for a prolonged period? If so, how did that length of time that you experienced the temptation or suffering affect your life?

3. How does hunger affect your decision-making, temper, or self-control? Considering this, how do you view Jesus' ability to resist the devil in this passage? (Keep in mind, Jesus wasn't just hungry from not eating breakfast. He hadn't eaten in forty days.)

4. With what was the devil trying to tempt Jesus in the following passages?

   Verse 3:

   Verses 6–7:

   Verses 9–11:

   Of these types of temptations, which one do you struggle with the most? Why?

5. Look at Scriptures that Jesus used to combat each temptation in verses 4, 8, and 12. In your own words, summarize the truth of these passages and how they helped Jesus to overcome each of the enemy's attacks.

   "Man shall not live on bread alone" (Deuteronomy 8:3).

"Worship the LORD your God and serve him only"
(Deuteronomy 6:13 NLT).

"Do not put the LORD your God to the test"
(Deuteronomy 6:16).

6. How do you think you would have handled this intense period of temptation? What would you have done similarly or differently to what Jesus did?

7. Read Hebrews 4:12. Do you ever use Scripture to help you fight temptation? How is the Word of God like a sharp and piercing sword?

8. Jesus was able to endure every attack from the enemy and not succumb to temptation. What are some of the ways that you think you might have handled this intense

period of temptation differently than Jesus? What does that realization inspire you to do?

Closing reflection: In light of today's passage, list any words or phrases that come to mind that describe Jesus' character. Pick one of these words or phrases and thank Jesus for being this way. Praise him for fighting on your behalf and defeating the devil in your place—and for offering his sinless life as a sacrifice for you on the cross. Ask him to make you more like him.

THE RETURN TO NAZARETH

If you're still not convinced that Jesus fully understood the challenges of life, all you need to do is look at what happened next when—after forty days of suffering and temptation in the wilderness—Jesus returned to his hometown of Nazareth. As Luke records:

> [16] *He went to Nazareth, where he had been brought up, and on the Sabbath day he went into the synagogue, as was his custom. He stood up to read,* [17] *and the scroll of the prophet Isaiah was handed to him. Unrolling it, he found the place where it is written:*
>
> > [18] *"The Spirit of the Lord is on me,*
> > *because he has anointed me*
> > *to proclaim good news to the poor.*

He has sent me to proclaim freedom for the prisoners
and recovery of sight for the blind,
to set the oppressed free,
19 to proclaim the year of the Lord's favor."

20 Then he rolled up the scroll, gave it back to the attendant
and sat down. The eyes of everyone in the synagogue were
fastened on him. 21 He began by saying to them, "Today this
scripture is fulfilled in your hearing."

22 All spoke well of him and were amazed at the gra-
cious words that came from his lips. "Isn't this Joseph's son?"
they asked (Luke 4:16–22).

1. What was the subject of Jesus' sermon to the people in Nazareth? How did the people respond?

2. The attitude of those in attendance quickly changed. As Luke tells us:

24 "Truly I tell you," he continued, "no prophet is accepted in
his hometown. 25 I assure you that there were many widows
in Israel in Elijah's time, when the sky was shut for three and
a half years and there was a severe famine throughout the
land. 26 Yet Elijah was not sent to any of them, but to a widow
in Zarephath in the region of Sidon. 27 And there were many
in Israel with leprosy in the time of Elisha the prophet, yet not
one of them was cleansed—only Naaman the Syrian."

²⁸ All the people in the synagogue were furious when they heard this. ²⁹ They got up, drove him out of the town, and took him to the brow of the hill on which the town was built, in order to throw him off the cliff. ³⁰ But he walked right through the crowd and went on his way (verses 24–30).

How did the people respond to this portion of Jesus' sermon passage? Why do you think they were so furious that they tried to kill Jesus?

3. Jesus referenced two stories in his sermon. The first is from 1 Kings 17:1–24, when Elijah took refuge with a widow in Zarephath during a severe famine. The second is found in 2 Kings 5:1–19, when Elisha healed a leper. These stories were controversial for Jesus' audience because both the widow and the leper were Gentiles. Why do you think Jesus followed up the passage in Isaiah with these stories? What message was he conveying?

4. We don't have a record of what Jesus thought or what he felt when the people took him to the cliff, intending to throw him off. Spend some time imagining that scene.

How do you think Jesus was feeling in that moment? How would you have felt?

5. Have you ever felt betrayed, misunderstood, or hurt by someone with whom you were close? What was that experience like for you? How did it affect your relationship with that person, or people, who hurt you?

6. Despite this experience in Nazareth, and others in which Jesus' friends and neighbors called him a lunatic or didn't believe him (see Mark 3:21), Jesus continued to spread the message that he had come to set the captives free. What does this tell you about Jesus' character? About his commitment to do God's will on earth?

Closing reflection: Whether you have been betrayed, hurt, misunderstood, or ostracized by those around you, Jesus understands what it feels like. As we saw in today's passage, the people in his hometown of Nazareth—friends, teachers, community leaders—tried to kill him. What hurt or pain do you need to bring to Christ today? Considering the stories you studied this week, how can Christ understand this particular hurt or pain?

Further Reflection

Reflect on what you studied this week: Adam and Eve's temptation in the Garden of Eden, Jesus' temptation in the wilderness, and the rejection that Christ experienced in Nazareth. Journal your thoughts on these topics or write them as a prayer to God, whether you need to ask him questions about what you learned, thank him for what you learned, or ask him what to do next now that you have a better understanding. Also write down any observations or questions that you want to bring to your next group time.

COMPASSIONATE PHYSICIAN

While Jesus was having dinner at Levi's house, many tax collectors and sinners were eating with him and his disciples, for there were many who followed him. When the teachers of the law who were Pharisees saw him eating with the sinners and tax collectors, they asked his disciples: "Why does he eat with tax collectors and sinners?" On hearing this, Jesus said to them, "It is not the healthy who need a doctor, but the sick. I have not come to call the righteous, but sinners."

MARK 2:15–17

OPENING REFLECTION

Everyone approaches prayer for healing a bit differently. Some are optimistic and hopeful, asking God for complete healing and believing that he will provide it. Others are skeptical, avoiding the prayer altogether and doing whatever they (and science) can to receive the healing they need. Many fall somewhere in the middle, not praying for healing but for the doctors, or praying for peace and comfort even if physical healing does not come.

Praying for healing is incredibly vulnerable because the risk is incredibly high. What if you pray the prayer . . . and it just doesn't work? What if God does *not* heal?

One of Jesus' divine qualities was as a compassionate physician. He healed those who were blind—including a man who had been blind since birth. He healed a woman who had been bleeding for twelve years and restored Peter's mother-in-law to health. He healed those afflicted with leprosy and gave those who were paralyzed the ability to walk. He performed many other miracles—including raising the dead to life.

But Jesus' healings were never just physical. As the blind man responded after Jesus healed him, "'Lord, I believe,' and he worshiped him" (John 9:38). Jesus healed both physically *and* spiritually.

The discomfort of physical sickness, the despair and pain that it causes, the isolation that it might cause—this makes us long for just the physical healing, whether it is for ourselves or someone else. But healing is required just as much for our hearts, which grow sick from sin, anger, depression, and a loss of hope. We need Jesus to heal us *completely*—not just physically.

So, how do we get this healing? How can we be touched by the divine? Well, we can take a tip from those who were on the receiving end of Jesus' healing miracles: *just ask.*

TALK ABOUT IT

Begin your group time by inviting anyone to share his or her insights from last week's personal study. Next, to get things started, discuss one of the following questions:

- Do you know someone, or have you ever heard the story of someone, who was miraculously healed from an illness?

— *or* —

- How do you approach praying for healing? Do you do it boldly or with certain reservations?

VIDEO TEACHING NOTES

Play the video segment for session three. As you watch, use the following outline to record any thoughts or concepts that stand out to you.

NOTES

Jesus went into the towns and countryside and *sought* those who had been affected by all forms of ailments—and healed them. He reached out to anyone in need. He is still willing to reach out in compassion to those who are suffering today.

Matthew describes how Jesus went up a mountainside and for three days was in the midst of every type of suffering. We have no record of preaching, teaching, or instructing during this time. Jesus is just there, with them, sharing in their pain.

In Jewish culture, sickness was viewed as a form of divine justice for sin. We know this because when the disciples walked by a man who had been blind since birth, they asked, "Rabbi, who sinned, this man or his parents?" (John 9:2 NASB).

Jesus heals the man. But he isn't content to just leave it there. He tracks him down. When the man sees him, his spiritual eyes are opened as well. He believes in Jesus and worships him. Jesus' healing is completed—both physically and spiritually.

As we look at these stories of healing in the Gospels, it's clear that Jesus understands our suffering, and that he will use our pain for a purpose. Our problems, struggles, heartaches, and hassles cooperate toward one end: the glory of God.

The story of the woman who had been bleeding for twelve years reveals that healing begins when we activtely *do* something. Healing begins when we reach out. Healing starts when we take a step.

This is a fallen world, and sickness and sin stalk our planet. But neither will have dominion over God's people. The very sin and sickness that Satan intends for evil God redeems for good. Sin becomes a showcase of his grace, and sickness becomes a demonstration of his ability to heal.

GROUP DISCUSSION

Take a few minutes with your group members to discuss what you just watched and explore these concepts in Scripture.

1. What has been your experience with illness, prayer, and God? What were you taught growing up about God's healing of the physical body in your church tradition or culture? How has this affected the way that you view God's ability to heal today?

2. Read Matthew 15:30–31. What type of illnesses did Jesus heal? How did the people respond? If you had been in the crowd that day, how might you have responded—with hope, amazement, skepticism, unbelief? Explain.

3. Read John 9:1–4. Which is tougher for you to accept: this man's condition or the realization it was God's idea? Do you think God causes some to be sick so that his works might be displayed in them? Why or why not?

4. Read Mark 5:25–34. What does Jesus say healed the woman? What role do you think faith plays in healing?

5. Read Jesus' statement about prayer to his disciples in Matthew 17:20. How could Jesus' words apply to when, how, and why you would pray for healing?

6. Jesus didn't *only* heal people physically. How else does he heal (see Matthew 15:31, Mark 5:29, and John 9:35–39)?

7. Do you agree that *healing begins when we reach out . . . when we take a step*? Why or why not? Of the people discussed in this week's teaching, which ones reached out for help? How did they do this?

8. Do you need physical or spiritual healing today? Or do you know someone else who does? After today's discussion, how do you feel about bringing that need to Jesus today in prayer?

CLOSING ACTIVITY

Briefly review the outline for the video teaching and any notes that you took. In the space below, write down what it means that God may heal you *instantly* or *gradually* . . . but always *ultimately*. How does this change your perspective on healing? How is praying for healing an act of obedience? If you feel comfortable, share what you have written with the rest of the group.

Closing Prayer

Spend some time as a group in contemplative prayer. Have someone guide you through the following thoughts, leaving a few moments of silence between each one: *"God, we thank you for your ability to heal. We confess we have not always had faith that you would make us well. We ask for healing for whoever comes to mind at this moment and ask that you would heal our hearts of sin. Give us faith when we have little. Give us healing physically, spiritually, and emotionally. In Jesus' name we pray, amen."* Following this, record any specific prayer requests from your group members, and then commit to praying for those requests throughout the week. Also record any praise reports that people have to share.

NAME   PRAYER REQUEST / PRAISE REPORT

BETWEEN-SESSIONS
PERSONAL STUDY

Reflect on the material you have covered during your group time by engaging in the following between-sessions activities. This week, you will look further into the topic of faith and healing, both physically and spiritually, as it is presented in the Bible. Each personal study consists of three days of reflection activities to help you implement what you learned in the group time. The time you invest will be well spent, so let God use it to draw you closer to him. At your next meeting, share any key points or insights that stood out to you as you spent this time with the Lord.

YE OF LITTLE,
NONE, OR A LOT OF FAITH

This week, you discussed the role of *faith* in healing. You looked at the story of the woman who had been bleeding for twelve years and how she sought out Jesus (in faith) for her healing. This raises a question: *What is the connection between faith and healing?* While the Bible is clear it is *God alone* who brings healing, faith definitely plays a role in how that healing can flow. Mark touches on this point in his Gospel when he relates the following story:

> ¹ *Jesus left there and went to his hometown, accompanied by his disciples.* ² *When the Sabbath came, he began to teach in the synagogue, and many who heard him were amazed.*
>
> *"Where did this man get these things?" they asked. "What's this wisdom that has been given him? What are these remarkable miracles he is performing?* ³ *Isn't this the carpenter? Isn't this Mary's son and the brother of James, Joseph, Judas and Simon? Aren't his sisters here with us?" And they took offense at him.*
>
> ⁴ *Jesus said to them, "A prophet is not without honor except in his own town, among his relatives and in his own home."* ⁵ *He could not do any miracles there, except lay his hands on a few sick people and heal them.* ⁶ *He was amazed at their lack of faith* (Mark 6:1–6).

1. What questions did the people in Nazareth ask about Jesus (see verses 2–3)?

2. How did Jesus respond to their skepticism of him (see verse 4)?

3. What do you learn in this passage about the connection between faith and miracles?

4. The people in Jesus' hometown of Nazareth had a great lack of faith in him. Others whom Jesus encountered demonstrated faith in varying degrees. The following is an example of one man who had at least a little faith in Christ:

> [20] *When the spirit saw Jesus, it immediately threw the boy into a convulsion. He fell to the ground and rolled around, foaming at the mouth.*
>
> [21] *Jesus asked the boy's father, "How long has he been like this?"*
>
> *"From childhood," he answered.* [22] *"It has often thrown him into fire or water to kill him. But if you can do anything, take pity on us and help us."*
>
> [23] *"'If you can'?" said Jesus. "Everything is possible for one who believes."*
>
> [24] *Immediately the boy's father exclaimed, "I do believe; help me overcome my unbelief!"*
>
> [25] *When Jesus saw that a crowd was running to the scene, he rebuked the impure spirit. "You deaf and mute spirit," he said, "I command you, come out of him and never enter him again."*
>
> [26] *The spirit shrieked, convulsed him violently and came out. The boy looked so much like a corpse that many said, "He's dead."* [27] *But Jesus took him by the hand and lifted him to his feet, and he stood up* (Mark 9:20–27).

What prompted Jesus to recognize the boy needed healing? What type of healing did this boy need from Jesus (see verses 20–21)?

5. What plea did the father make to Jesus? How did Jesus respond (see verses 22–23)?

6. What did the boy's father confess about his amount of faith (see verse 24)?

7. If Jesus were standing before you right now, would you be able to boldly profess your complete faith in him and in God's power to heal? Why or why not?

8. How would you assess the overall strength of your faith in God today? What experiences have bolstered or reduced your faith in God's power to work miracles?

Closing reflection: Talk to Jesus about your level of faith in him. If you're having a hard time trusting in him or his power right now, follow the example of the man with the demon-possessed son and simply say, "I believe; help my unbelief!" Consciously look for instances throughout your day where you see God answering this prayer.

THE LORD LOOKS AT THE HEART

Jesus' healing was not superficial. He healed physically *and* spiritually, which reflects a consistent theme in Scripture—that God looks at the heart, not the outward appearance. Consider the following verses that show it is the attitude of the *heart* that matters to God.

1. "The LORD does not look at the things people look at. People look at the outward appearance, but the LORD looks at the heart" (1 Samuel 16:7). How do people judge one another? How does God judge us?

2. "Keep your heart with all vigilance, for from it flow the springs of life" (Proverbs 4:23 NRSV). What does it mean that the "springs of life" flow from the heart?

3. "I the LORD search the heart and examine the mind, to reward each person according to their conduct, according to what their deeds deserve" (Jeremiah 17:10). What does this verse say is important to God? How does he reward us?

4. "Blessed are the pure in heart, for they will see God" (Matthew 5:8). How would you define the "pure in heart"? How does this allow a person to clearly see God?

5. "The good person out of the good treasure of his heart produces good, and the evil person out of his evil treasure produces evil, for out of the abundance of the heart his mouth speaks" (Luke 6:45 ESV). What is the link between the "treasure" that is stored in the heart and the way that a person speaks and acts?

6. If the Bible talks so much about the state of the heart, why do you think so many people today focus on the exterior—on physical health, looks, our superficial qualities?

7. When was the last time you examined your heart? If you are not sure, spend some time examining the health of your heart. Check any statements that apply to you:

❏ I've had judgmental thoughts toward a friend.
❏ I've said unkind words to someone I love.
❏ I've been harsh and judgmental toward myself.
❏ I've felt angry, sad, depressed, or anxious.

How do you feel about the current state of your heart?

8. Considering these verses as a whole, how important is the heart to God? Given this, why do you think Jesus chose to heal people *spiritually* and *physically*?

Closing reflection: As you think about one of the behaviors you checked above, invite Jesus to come into your heart and heal whatever is at the source of the problem. Or, if you are experiencing anxiety, depression, or sadness, ask Jesus to bring you comfort and help in your time of need. Ask the Lord to show you a friend or family member in whom you can confide and who can help you in your journey toward healing.

WAITING FOR HEALING

If you are a believer in Christ, your highest certainty is that God will heal you *ultimately*. In heaven, the Lord will restore your body to its intended splendor. As John wrote, "We know that when Christ appears, we shall be like him" (1 John 3:2).

Where are you in your healing journey? Are you still waiting to be healed? Have you been healed? Are you waiting for someone else to be healed? It can be difficult when you find yourself in the place between the diagnosis and the cure. If this describes your current condition, you may want to take a cue from the prophet Habakkuk.

God had given Habakkuk a vision. The Israelites would be punished for their wicked ways by being taken into captivity by the Babylonians. God would eventually deliver them, but Habakkuk didn't know when that would happen. While he was wrestling with this unknown, he assumed four postures: *questioning, waiting, remembrance,* and *praise.*

QUESTIONING

1. Read Habakkuk 1:2-7. How would you describe the nature of Habakkuk's questions to God (see verses 2–4)?

2. How would you describe the nature of God's reply to Habakkuk (see verses 5–7)? How do you think Habakkuk would have felt about this response?

WAITING

3. Read Habakkuk 2:1–4. What does Habakkuk resolve to do in these verses?

4. What does God say about his timing? What reason does God give Habakkuk to keep waiting (see verses 3–4)?

REMEMBRANCE

5. Next, the prophet spends time in remembrance, calling to mind the many attributes of God. Read Habakkuk 3:3–6. What kind of God is Habakkuk describing here?

6. Why do you think he was moved to remember the character of God at this point?

PRAISE

7. Habakkuk's final posture is one of praise. Read Habakkuk 3:17–19. What sort of landscape is Habakkuk looking at when he praises the Lord?

8. Why do you think Habakkuk was able to praise God even though "the fig tree does not blossom, and no fruit is on the vines"?

Closing reflection: Where do you find yourself in Habakkuk's story? Are you at the stage of *questioning* God, *waiting* on God, *remembering* God, or *praising* God? Take a moment to identify where you are and why you are there. Perhaps you've been in this posture for too long and it's time to move to the next phase. Or maybe you are trying to force yourself into a posture of praise when you really need to ask more questions or you need to remain waiting. Take a moment to assess what you need right now in your journey toward healing—to move forward or to stay put. Wherever you are, approach the throne of God in that posture. Be honest. If you are questioning, ask him your questions. If you are remembering his faithfulness, thank him for what he's done. If you are ready to praise him, do so wholeheartedly.

FURTHER REFLECTION

Reflect on what you studied this week: the faith of people in Jesus' day, the importance God places on the heart, and the postures to assume as you wait for God's healing. Journal your thoughts on these topics or write them as a prayer to God, whether you need to ask him questions about what you learned, thank him for what you learned, or ask him what to do next now that you have a better understanding. Also write down any observations or questions that you want to bring to your next group time.

GREAT TEACHER

Coming to his hometown, he began teaching the people in their synagogue, and they were amazed. "Where did this man get this wisdom and these miraculous powers?" they asked. "Isn't this the carpenter's son? Isn't his mother's name Mary. . . . And they took offense at him. But Jesus said to them, "A prophet is not without honor except in his own town and in his own home." And he did not do many miracles there because of their lack of faith.

MATTHEW 13:54–58

OPENING REFLECTION

We all live within a system of power. Whether you live in a democracy, a republic, or a kingdom, you live under the rule of a president, king, queen, parliamentary leader, or other form of government. These systems of power create a hierarchy in society, where some have more influence than others. As a result, some are considered to have more value.

But when Jesus came to this earth, he instituted a completely different system of power—one in which hierarchy does not determine value but all are considered equal. Under this system, ultimate power and authority are in the hands of the kindest and most generous leader who ever lived. This is God's kingdom, and Jesus' primary job was to bring it to earth.

When Jesus quoted the prophet Isaiah at the beginning of his ministry, he laid out the basic principles of this kingdom: "The Spirit of the LORD is upon Me, because He has anointed Me to preach the gospel to the poor; He has sent Me to heal the brokenhearted. To proclaim liberty to the captives and recovery of sight to the blind, to set at liberty those who are oppressed; to proclaim the acceptable year of the LORD" (Luke 4:18-19 NKJV).

The kingdom of God would not elevate the rich, the healthy, or the powerful. In fact, it would do the opposite. It would care for the poor, heal the broken, and free the enslaved. The kingdom of God was good news for everyone, but it was even better news for the marginalized. Furthermore, this kingdom was not some far-off system to be realized in the future. As Jesus said, "Your kingdom *come*, your will be done" (Matthew 6:10).

Christ brought God's kingdom to earth. He was the embodiment of it. For this reason, we are already living in God's kingdom. These principles apply to us and those around us. The truth Jesus brought is the same for us today: We are healed. We are accepted. We are free.

TALK ABOUT IT

Begin your group time by inviting anyone to share his or her insights from last week's personal study. Next, to get things started, discuss one of the following questions:

- Who is the best teacher that you had growing up? What made that person's teachings especially memorable to you?

— or —

- Would you consider yourself more of a rule follower or rule breaker? Why? Have you always been this way?

VIDEO TEACHING NOTES

Play the video segment for session four. As you watch, use the following outline to record any thoughts or concepts that stand out to you.

NOTES

When Jesus announced God's kingdom had arrived, it came along with the offer of rest. Instead of piling on more rules, Jesus offered a *relationship*. It is an offer that still stands today.

Jesus knew his mission. Early on, we find him in Nazareth, delivering his inaugural address about that mission. The people live in expectation of the coming Messiah—a Messiah who will purify the land and free them from foreign rule.

Jesus declares his mission: *Preach the gospel to the poor. Heal the brokenhearted. Proclaim liberty to the captives and recovery of sight to the blind. Set at liberty those who are oppressed.* It's not what people are expecting—not even John the Baptist.

Jesus describes a heavenly kingdom being established. A unique kingdom. An invisible kingdom. A kingdom where, first of all, *the rejected are received.* It's a point Jesus illustrates in a parables about a rich man and a beggar named Lazarus.

The second characteristic is that the *dead are raised to life.* The grave has no power over those who gain entrance into God's kingdom—and it's never too late to join. Jesus captures this theme in a story about a landowner who needs some workers.

The third truth is that *the good news is proclaimed to the poor.* In God's kingdom, membership is *granted*, not *purchased.* We gain entrance not by attempting to do enough but by admitting we *can't* do enough. We are all lost until God finds us.

The older brother represents the Pharisees in Jesus' day. They were the authorities. They were right. And they knew it. Jesus had no patience for this way of thinking, but had patience for those who were earnestly seeking the truth.

Jesus' conversation with Nicodemus led John to write the Hope diamond of the Bible: "For God so loved the world that he gave his one and only Son, that whoever believes in him shall not perish but have eternal life" (John 3:16). God loves. He gave. We believe. We live.

GROUP DISCUSSION

Take a few minutes with your group members to discuss what you just watched and explore these concepts in Scripture.

1. Read Luke 4:18–19. Jesus quoted the prophet Isaiah in these verses, but to what was he actually referring? What type of kingdom does Jesus describe?

2. How does God's kingdom compare to our society today? What makes someone acceptable according to the standards and rules of the culture around us?

3. In God's kingdom, *the rejected are received.* How do you respond to the idea that God takes you as he finds you—no need to clean up or climb up, but only look up?

4. In God's kingdom, *the dead are raised to life.* It's never too late, and no one is too far gone, to receive God's salvation. How does this offer hope to you today—both for yourself and for your loved ones who have not yet found Christ?

5. In God's kingdom, *the good news is proclaimed to the poor.* In God's kingdom, membership is *granted*, not *purchased.* How does the story of the prodigal son illustrate how God receives those who have rebelled against him?

6. What does the story of the prodigal son say about those who try to "earn" their way into God's kingdom? In what ways are we all like both sons in the story?

7. Read John 3:1–16. What was Nicodemus' question for Jesus? How did Jesus respond? What question would you ask Jesus about the kingdom of God?

8. Why do you think Jesus agreed to meet with Nicodemus? What does this say about the way that Jesus will respond to each of us when we earnestly seek his truth?

CLOSING ACTIVITY

Briefly review the outline for the video teaching and any notes that you took. In the space below, write down what it means that you must be *born again* to enter into God's kingdom. What questions does this raise within you . . . like it raised within Nicodemus? Where in your life are you relying more on the muscle of self rather than the miracle of God? If you feel comfortable, share what you have written with the rest of the group.

CLOSING PRAYER

End your group time by praying the Lord's Prayer: *"Our Father in heaven, hallowed be your name, your kingdom come, your will be done, on earth as it is in heaven. Give us today our daily bread. And forgive us our debts, as we also have forgiven our debtors. And lead us not into temptation, but deliver us from the evil one"* (Matthew 6:9-13). In the space below, record any prayer requests or praise reports that your group members have to share.

NAME   PRAYER REQUEST / PRAISE REPORT

BETWEEN-SESSIONS
PERSONAL STUDY

Reflect on the material you have covered during your group time by engaging in the following between-sessions activities. This week, you will take a closer look at the three parables of Jesus that were during this session. Each personal study consists of three days of reflection activities to help you implement what you learned in the group time. The time you invest will be well spent, so let God use it to draw you closer to him. At your next meeting, share any key points or insights that stood out to you as you spent this time with the Lord.

THE REJECTED ARE RECEIVED

This week, you looked at three characteristics of the kingdom of God that Jesus presented in the Gospels. The first characteristic is that *the rejected are received*. To illustrate this point, you looked at a parable that Jesus told about a rich man and a poor man named Lazarus. Before you study the parable, answer the following questions:

1. What do you think makes a person valuable? What do you think makes *you* valuable?

2. Now read the parable that Jesus told:

> [19] "There was a rich man who was dressed in purple and fine linen and lived in luxury every day. [20] At his gate was laid a beggar named Lazarus, covered with sores [21] and longing to eat what fell from the rich man's table. Even the dogs came and licked his sores.
>
> [22] "The time came when the beggar died and the angels carried him to Abraham's side. The rich man also died and was buried. [23] In Hades, where he was in torment, he looked up and saw Abraham far away, with Lazarus by his side. [24] So he called to him, 'Father Abraham, have pity on me and send Lazarus to dip the tip of his finger in water and cool my tongue, because I am in agony in this fire.'
>
> [25] "But Abraham replied, 'Son, remember that in your lifetime you received your good things, while Lazarus received bad things, but now he is comforted here and you are in agony. [26] And besides all this, between us and you a great chasm has been set in place so that those who want to go from here to you cannot, nor can anyone cross over from there to us.'
>
> [27] "He answered, 'Then I beg you, father, send Lazarus to my family, [28] for I have five brothers. Let him warn them, so that they will not also come to this place of torment.'

[29] *"Abraham replied, 'They have Moses and the Prophets; let them listen to them.'*

[30] *"'No, father Abraham,' he said, 'but if someone from the dead goes to them, they will repent.'*

[31] *"He said to him, 'If they do not listen to Moses and the Prophets, they will not be convinced even if someone rises from the dead'"* (Luke 16:19–31).

How would you describe the rich man? How would you describe the poor man named Lazarus (see verses 19–21)?

3. How does Lazarus feel in the afterlife? How does the rich man feel (see verse 25)?

4. Why do you think Lazarus and the rich man ended up where they did after they died?

5. What does the rich man beg Abraham to do? Why doesn't Abraham do it (see verses 27–29)?

6. What does Abraham mean when he says, "If they do not listen to Moses and the Prophets, they will not be convinced even if someone rises from the dead" (verse 31)?

7. What does this parable teach about what makes a person righteous and worthy of entering into God's kingdom?

8. Jesus' parable paints a somber picture of the rich man's fate. How do you feel about this story? Does anything bother you, confuse you, or make you uncomfortable? If so, why do you think that part, or parts, of the story are difficult for you to comprehend?

Closing reflection: Close your time in the Word today by reading the Beatitudes found in Matthew 5:3–10. Ask Jesus to help you see others through the lens of God's kingdom—

where the last are first and the meek are blessed. Also thank him for the promise that all are welcome into his kingdom... and that status or position don't matter to God.

THE DEAD ARE RAISED TO LIFE

The second characteristic of the kingdom of God is that "the dead are raised to life" (Matthew 11:5 NCV). Death—typically considered the ultimate end—has no power over those who are in God's kingdom. God extends the offer of eternal life to all who accept Jesus as their Savior, regardless of their current situation in life or what they have done in the past. To illustrate this point, you looked at a parable that Jesus told about a landowner and some workers he hired. Before you study the parable, answer the following questions:

1. Generally speaking, do you believe you've gotten what you've deserved in life? Why or why not?

2. Now read the parable that Jesus told:

1" For the kingdom of heaven is like a landowner who went out early in the morning to hire workers for his vineyard. 2 He agreed to pay them a denarius for the day and sent them into his vineyard.

93

³ *"About nine in the morning he went out and saw others standing in the marketplace doing nothing.* ⁴ *He told them, 'You also go and work in my vineyard, and I will pay you whatever is right.'* ⁵ *So they went.*

"He went out again about noon and about three in the afternoon and did the same thing. ⁶ *About five in the afternoon he went out and found still others standing around. He asked them, 'Why have you been standing here all day long doing nothing?'*

⁷ *"'Because no one has hired us,' they answered.*

"He said to them, 'You also go and work in my vineyard.'

⁸ *"When evening came, the owner of the vineyard said to his foreman, 'Call the workers and pay them their wages, beginning with the last ones hired and going on to the first.'*

⁹ *"The workers who were hired about five in the afternoon came and each received a denarius.* ¹⁰ *So when those came who were hired first, they expected to receive more. But each one of them also received a denarius.* ¹¹ *When they received it, they began to grumble against the landowner.* ¹² *'These who were hired last worked only one hour,' they said, 'and you have made them equal to us who have borne the burden of the work and the heat of the day.'*

¹³ *"But he answered one of them, 'I am not being unfair to you, friend. Didn't you agree to work for a denarius?* ¹⁴ *Take your pay and go. I want to give the one who was hired last the same as I gave you.* ¹⁵ *Don't I have the right to do what I want with my own money? Or are you envious because I am generous?'*

¹⁶ *"So the last will be first, and the first will be last"* (Matthew 20:1–16).

At what times of day did the landowner hire workers to work his vineyard (see verses 3, 5–6)? Who do these different groups of workers represent?

1. What did the workers who had been hired earlier in the day expect to receive? Why do you think they had these expectations (see verse 10)?

2. What did the disgruntled workers say to the landowner when they learned he was paying everyone the same? How does the landowner respond (see verses 12–15)?

3. Have you ever been jealous of someone who got an opportunity, a raise, a relationship, or something else that you felt you deserved? If so, explain the situation. Why did you feel you deserved what this person received?

4. According to this parable, who *deserved* to be paid one denarius at the end of the day?

5. What does this message say about God's kingdom? What does this message say about the character of Jesus?

6. What points of tension do you feel with this parable? What is unsettling about it, convicting, or confusing? Spend some time writing down your thoughts.

Closing reflection: Think about how you answered the first question as to whether you believe that you've gotten what you've deserved in life. After today's study, would you answer this question any differently—especially when you consider that you are a member of the five o'clock workers? Also bring any concern or confusion you might have about this teaching to Jesus in prayer. Ask him to help you see what you and others deserve based on the principles of God's kingdom—rather than your own.

THE GOOD NEWS
IS PROCLAIMED TO ALL

The third characteristic of God's kingdom is that "The good news is proclaimed to the poor" (Matthew 11:5). It is not just the rich, powerful, or popular who get to partake in the good news of the kingdom, but also the lowliest on the social and economic ladders. To illustrate this point, you looked at a parable that Jesus told about two sons.

You are probably familiar with this one. The story begins with a reckless and thankless son who asks his father for his inheritance so he can blow it on wild living. However, when the party is over and the son finds he is broke, he quickly regrets his decision. He decides to return home and beg his father to be one of his servants. But his father is so pleased to have his son back that he welcomes him with open arms. This is the character we talk about the most—the "prodigal son." But there is another son in the story:

> [25] *"Meanwhile, the older son was in the field. When he came near the house, he heard music and dancing.* [26] *So he called one of the servants and asked him what was going on.* [27] *'Your brother has come,' he replied, 'and your father has killed the fattened calf because he has him back safe and sound.'*
>
> [28] *"The older brother became angry and refused to go in. So his father went out and pleaded with him.* [29] *But he answered his father, 'Look! All these years I've been slaving for you and never disobeyed your orders. Yet you never gave me even a young goat so I could celebrate with my friends.* [30] *But when this son of yours who has squandered your property with prostitutes comes home, you kill the fattened calf for him!'*

> [31] "'My son,' the father said, 'you are always with me, and everything I have is yours. [32] But we had to celebrate and be glad, because this brother of yours was dead and is alive again; he was lost and is found'" (Luke 15:25–32).

1. How did the older brother feel about the celebration of his younger brother's return (see verse 28)?

2. How does the father respond to the older brother (see verse 28)?

3. What was the older brother's complaint? What did he say that he had done while the younger brother was off enjoying his wild living (see verse 29)?

4. In the parable of the landowner, the worker's complaint was about the amount of time they had worked. How is the older son's complaint similar? How is it different?

5. How does the father respond to his older son's complaint (see verses 31–32)? What stands out to you about what he says? How does he describe the younger son?

6. What does the father's response tell you about the way he feels for *all* his children—regardless of whether they are more like the younger or the older son?

Closing reflection: Think about who you identify with more — the prodigal son or the older brother. Considering how the father treated both sons regardless of their actions or attitudes, and that you have been adopted into his family, how do you think God feels about *you?* End your time in silent prayer. Listen for the loving voice of God to speak to you.

FURTHER REFLECTION

Reflect on what you studied this week about the kingdom of God: it is a place where the rejected are received, the dead are raised to life, and the good news is proclaimed to all. Journal your thoughts on these topics or write them as a prayer to God, whether you need to ask him questions about what you learned, thank him for what you learned, or ask him what to do next now that you have a better understanding. Also write down any observations or questions that you want to bring to your next group time.

MIRACLE WORKER

*As evening approached, the disciples came to him and said,
"This is a remote place, and it's already getting late. Send the crowds
away, so they can go to the villages and buy themselves some food."
Jesus replied, "They do not need to go away. You give them something
to eat." "We have here only five loaves of bread and two fish," they
answered. "Bring them here to me," he said. . . . Taking the five
loaves and the two fish and looking up to heaven, he gave thanks
and broke the loaves. Then he gave them to the disciples, and the
disciples gave them to the people.*

MATTHEW 14:15–19

OPENING REFLECTION

When you're hungry, and food is available, you eat. When you're sick, and healthcare is available, you go to a doctor or take medication. If you have a car and it breaks down, you go to a mechanic to get it fixed. We all generally know where to go to have our basic needs met.

When Jesus was on this earth, he spent three years meeting the needs of those around him. He offered physical and spiritual healing to those who came seeking it. He saved the disciples from capsizing on the Sea of Galilee. He turned water into wine. He proved again and again that he can—and will—meet our needs. The question is, *Will we ask him to do so?*

Even though Jesus' disciples walked with him for three years and witnessed his power daily, they still doubted Jesus' ability to meet their needs. In fact, on one occasion, before Jesus turned a few pieces of bread into a feast for a crowd, his disciples doubted his ability to do it. They preferred he dismiss the hungry multitude rather than help them—complaining the crowd was too big and the need too great.

But it was not for Jesus. He prayed to the Father, and the next thing the twelve disciples and thousands of others knew, they were all being fed from a young boy's lunch. As John records, "When they had all had enough to eat, [Jesus] said to his disciples, 'Gather the pieces that are left over. Let nothing be wasted.' So they gathered them and filled twelve baskets with the pieces of the five barley loaves left over by those who had eaten" (John 6:12–13).

Jesus not only met the needs of the crowd but also *exceeded* them. And he can—and will—do the same in our lives today. So today as you begin this study, consider what is your greatest need. Do you trust in Jesus' ability to meet it? Have you asked him to do so?

TALK ABOUT IT

Begin your group time by inviting anyone to share his or her insights from last week's personal study. Next, to get things started, discuss one of the following questions:

- When was the last time you prayed about something you needed? If you feel comfortable sharing, what was the need you prayed for?

— *or* —

- What is the most miraculous answer that you have received for prayer that you or someone you know prayed?

VIDEO TEACHING NOTES

Play the video segment for session five. As you watch, use the following outline to record any thoughts or concepts that stand out to you.

NOTES

Need some help with anxiety? Need some reassurance that God understands what you need?

Look no further than to the life of Jesus. He showed time and again that God not only knows what we need but can—and *will*—provide for us when we trust in him.

Jesus showed us that God cares about our needs in the greatest storms of life. One time, the disciples found themselves in a storm on the Sea of Galilee, and they feared for their lives. But Jesus simply said, "Quiet! Be still!" If he can calm the raging seas, he can calm any tempest in our lives.

Jesus showed us that God cares about our needs in the little areas of life. At a wedding in Cana, a bride and groom ran out of wine—and there was no way to sweep the embarrassment under the rug. Jesus' mother simply took the problem to him and said, "They have no more wine."

Jesus didn't change the water to wine to impress the crowd or get the wedding master's attention. Jesus performed the miracle simply because his friends were embarrassed. What bothered them bothered him. The same is true for us today.

Later, Jesus ministered to the needs of a multitude of people. When it got late, *the followers came to him* and told Jesus to dismiss the people. They didn't consult Christ, just described all the problems. Their words imply an adjourned meeting.

The boy with the sack lunch wrestled with the silliness of it all. But he gave the lunch to Jesus. Something told him if he planted the seed, God would grant the crop. Jesus took the lunch, thanked God, and then fed the entire crowd with it.

Had Jesus acted according to the disciples' faith, the multitudes would have gone unfed. But he didn't then . . . and he doesn't today. He is true to us even when we forget him.

Worry comes with life. But it doesn't have to take your life. During Jesus' time on earth, he assured us that we don't need to be consumed by anxiety, because God will always provide for our needs when we come to him with our requests.

GROUP DISCUSSION

Take a few minutes with your group members to discuss what you just watched and explore these concepts in Scripture.

1. Jesus spent thirty-three years on earth, but only three of those years were spent doing ministry. Why do you think Jesus spent the additional thirty years in this world?

2. Read Mark 4:35–41. If you were a disciple on the boat, how would you have reacted to the storm? How would you have reacted to Jesus' calming the storm?

3. Jesus' calming of the storm reveals there is no problem too large for God to solve. When have you seen this to be true in your life? What are some other miracles you have read about in the Bible that reveal God is all-powerful over every situation?

4. Read John 2:1–10. Why do you think Jesus chose to intervene in this situation? When have you seen God intervene in the "small things" in your life?

5. What can you learn in the story from Mary's example? When you have a need or feel anxious or afraid, why is it important to go *first* to Jesus?

6. In the story, we see that God provides the miracle—turning the water to wine—when the people do what Jesus instructs them to do. Have you ever experienced this in your life—obedience leading to abundance? If so, what was that experience like for you?

7. On the other hand, have you ever been obedient to God and not received the abundance you thought you would? If so, what was that experience like for you?

8. In the story of the feeding of the five thousand, how do you think the boy felt in offering up his small lunch to Jesus? Why do you think God often puts us in similar situations when it comes to offering up the resources we have for his use?

CLOSING ACTIVITY

Briefly review the outline for the video teaching and any notes you took. In the space below, write down one specific need that you would like to bring to God. How do the stories you heard in the teaching reveal that your need is not too large or too small for God? What do you need to do to trust that he will provide? How will you put the problem in Jesus' hands like Mary did? If you feel comfortable, share what you have written with the rest of the group.

CLOSING PRAYER

Spend some time sharing needs and prayer requests in the group, and then write these down in the space below (along with any praise reports the members have to share). You can either pray for the needs of each member of your group or you can leave a minute of silence for members of the group to individually bring their needs to Jesus. Regardless, commit to continue praying for these requests throughout the week.

NAME   PRAYER REQUEST / PRAISE REPORT

BETWEEN-SESSIONS
PERSONAL STUDY

Reflect on the material you have covered during your group time by engaging in the following between-sessions activities. This week, you will take a closer look at the story of Jesus' feeding the five thousand by considering three different perspectives from the characters involved. Each personal study consists of three days of reflection activities to help you implement what you learned in the group time. The time you invest will be well spent, so let God use it to draw you closer to him. At your next meeting, share any key points or insights that stood out to you as you spent this time with the Lord.

THE DISCIPLES

Other than Jesus, we find there were three main characters (or sets of characters) involved in the miracle of the feeding of the five thousand. For today's study, you will look more closely at how the *disciples* acted during this miracle, how Jesus responded to them, and the times in your life when you've had a similar attitude toward Jesus' ability to meet your needs. Read the following story as it is told in the Gospel of John:

¹Some time after this, Jesus crossed to the far shore of the Sea of Galilee (that is, the Sea of Tiberias), ² and a great crowd of people followed him because they saw the signs he had performed by healing the sick. ³ Then Jesus went up on a mountainside and sat down with his disciples. ⁴ The Jewish Passover Festival was near.

⁵ When Jesus looked up and saw a great crowd coming toward him, he said to Philip, "Where shall we buy bread for these people to eat?" ⁶ He asked this only to test him, for he already had in mind what he was going to do.

⁷ Philip answered him, "It would take more than half a year's wages to buy enough bread for each one to have a bite!"

⁸ Another of his disciples, Andrew, Simon Peter's brother, spoke up, ⁹ "Here is a boy with five small barley loaves and two small fish, but how far will they go among so many?"

¹⁰ Jesus said, "Have the people sit down." There was plenty of grass in that place, and they sat down (about five thousand men were there). ¹¹ Jesus then took the loaves, gave thanks, and distributed to those who were seated as much as they wanted. He did the same with the fish.

¹² When they had all had enough to eat, he said to his disciples, "Gather the pieces that are left over. Let nothing be wasted." ¹³ So they gathered them and filled twelve baskets with the pieces of the five barley loaves left over by those who had eaten.

¹⁴ After the people saw the sign Jesus performed, they began to say, "Surely this is the Prophet who is to come into the world" (John 6:1–14).

1. Why did the masses of people follow Jesus and the disciples to the shore of the Sea of Galilee? How did Jesus respond when he saw them gathered there?

2. What question did Jesus ask the disciples? How did Philip respond (see verses 5–7)?

3. What did Andrew then add to the discussion? What was his concern (see verses 8–9)?

4. It appears that Jesus already had in mind what he was going to do with the five loaves and two fish (see verse 6). If this was the case, why do you think he involved the disciples at all in the miracle?

5. Have you ever asked God for something that he did not provide for you? If so, what did you ask for? How did God's response, or lack thereof, affect your faith?

6. Have you ever asked God for something that he did provide? What was it? How did his provision affect you?

7. Do you tend to be skeptical of Jesus' ability to meet your needs? If so, describe a recent example. Why was it difficult to have faith in this situation?

8. In spite of the disciples' skepticism, Jesus provided for the crowd. Rather than *punish* the disciples, he *employed* them in passing out the bread and fish. What does this tell you about the character of Christ? How does Jesus' response make you feel about your moments of skepticism?

Closing reflection: Where do you fall today on the spectrum of fervent believer and skeptic? Tell Jesus where you are. You don't have to ask him for more faith, repent, or apologize. Simply tell him how you feel at this moment. Let an honest conversation unfold between you.

THE BOY

In the story of the feeding of the five thousand, it is the boy who actually surfaces as the hero. All he does is give his lunch to Jesus and leave the problem in Christ's hands. In many ways, he demonstrates the same faith that Mary showed when she left the problem of the bride and groom running out of wine in Jesus' hands. Read the following account of the story as it is told in the Gospel of Mark and consider what the boy's offering to Jesus reveals about our offerings:

> [35] *By this time it was late in the day, so his disciples came to him. "This is a remote place," they said, "and it's already very late.* [36] *Send the people away so that they can go to the surrounding countryside and villages and buy themselves something to eat."*
>
> [37] *But he answered, "You give them something to eat."*
>
> *They said to him, "That would take more than half a year's wages! Are we to go and spend that much on bread and give it to them to eat?"*
>
> [38] *"How many loaves do you have?" he asked. "Go and see."*
>
> *When they found out, they said, "Five—and two fish."*
>
> [39] *Then Jesus directed them to have all the people sit down in groups on the green grass.* [40] *So they sat down in groups of hundreds and fifties.* [41] *Taking the five loaves and the two fish and looking up to heaven, he gave thanks and broke the loaves. Then he gave them to his disciples to distribute to the people.*

He also divided the two fish among them all. ⁴² They all ate and were satisfied, ⁴³ and the disciples picked up twelve basketfuls of broken pieces of bread and fish. ⁴⁴ The number of the men who had eaten was five thousand (Mark 6:35–44).

1. What was the disciples' solution to the problem of feeding the people (see verses 35–36)?

2. Notice that Mark states Jesus sent the disciples out to take an inventory of their resources (see verse 38). Why do you think he did this?

3. Imagine this scene as vividly as you can. How old is the boy who gives the disciples the five loaves and two fish? What does he look like? What does he say when he shows the disciples the lunch he has packed?

4. Mark states that five-thousand *men* were gathered there that day. This number did not include the women and the children who were also present. If you factored them in, the crowd could have been as large as twenty-thousand people—the size of a small city.[1] How does this

change or affect the way you view this miracle and the boy's offering?

5. In our human limitation, we often feel helpless in the face of our problems. We have five barley loaves and two fish . . . but twenty-thousand mouths to feed. Do you think the boy thought his lunch would go so far? Why do you think he offered it anyway?

6. Jesus said, "Unless you change and become like little children, you will never enter the kingdom of heaven" (Matthew 18:3). Why do we all need to have childlike faith at times like the boy in this story demonstrated?

7. The boy in this story brought a simple offering to Jesus of five loaves and two fish. It wasn't much . . . but it was all he had. As we read in the Bible, "People look at the outward appearance, but the LORD looks at the heart" (1 Samuel 16:7). King David understood it is the condition of the heart that matters when he wrote:

> [16]*You do not delight in sacrifice, or I would bring it;*
> *you do not take pleasure in burnt offerings.*

¹⁷ *My sacrifice, O God, is a broken spirit;*
   a broken and contrite heart
   you, God, will not despise (Psalm 51:16–17).

David wrote these words after he was caught in the sin of adultery and abuse of power. What did he bring in this psalm as an offering to God?

8. According to David, how will God feel about this offering when you bring it to him?

Closing reflection: Go back to the overwhelming problem that you identified above—the one in which you feel helpless in the face of today. How could you offer this need to Jesus in the same way David brought his offering to God? Remember, David was in a dark place when he wrote these words. How could this bring you comfort in your own need today?

THE HUNGRY

We don't know the names of any of the 5,000-plus people that Jesus fed that day. They were simply "the crowd," yet in many ways they represent each of us. They came to Jesus for healing, and he healed them. They grew hungry, and he fed them. Read the story one last time, this time from the book of Matthew, and see what you can learn from the crowd who gathered on that historic day:

> [13] *When Jesus heard what had happened, he withdrew by boat privately to a solitary place. Hearing of this, the crowds followed him on foot from the towns.* [14] *When Jesus landed and saw a large crowd, he had compassion on them and healed their sick.*
>
> [15] *As evening approached, the disciples came to him and said, "This is a remote place, and it's already getting late. Send the crowds away, so they can go to the villages and buy themselves some food."*
>
> [16] *Jesus replied, "They do not need to go away. You give them something to eat."*
>
> [17] *"We have here only five loaves of bread and two fish," they answered.*
>
> [18] *"Bring them here to me," he said.* [19] *And he directed the people to sit down on the grass. Taking the five loaves and the two fish and looking up to heaven, he gave thanks and broke the loaves. Then he gave them to the disciples, and the disciples gave them to the people.* [20] *They all ate and were satisfied, and the disciples picked up twelve basketfuls of broken pieces that were left over.* [21] *The number of those who ate was about five thousand men, besides women and children* (Matthew 14:13–21).

1. Matthew tells us that Jesus had just learned of the death of John the Baptist when this scene unfolds (see Matthew 14:1–12), which is why he withdrew to a solitary place.

What did the crowds do when they found out where Jesus had gone (see verse 13)?

2. How did Jesus feel when he saw the crowds—in spite of what he had been dealing with that day? How did he respond (see verse 14)?

3. What did the disciples want to do with the crowd when it grew late? How did that compare to what Jesus wanted to do with them (see verses 15–16)?

4. How many people in the crowd got to eat? How did they feel after they ate (see verse 20)?

5. We can learn a lot about how Jesus wants to interact with us based on how he interacted with the crowd on that

day. Based on your answers to the questions above, what are we called to do when we have a need? How will Jesus respond to that?

6. What can you do to remember to—or be willing to—go to Jesus *first* in your time of need, as the crowd of people did in this story?

7. What could help you to better trust that Jesus will have compassion on you when you come to him, just as Jesus had compassion on the crowd?

8. Who in your life can you help to see that Jesus will provide for their needs—just as he miraculously multiplied the bread and fish for the crowd?

Closing reflection: In what is called the Lord's Prayer, Jesus said, "Give us today our daily bread" (Matthew 6:11). He did not ask for *monthly* bread or *annual* bread. He simply asked for the bread he needed to get through the day. What do you need from your heavenly Father to get through today? Ask him for it in the same way Jesus did: *Give me today my daily bread.*

FURTHER REFLECTION

Reflect on what you studied this week: the disciples' lack of faith in this story, the boy's simple faith in putting his lunch in Jesus' hands, and the way Jesus reacted to the needs of the people when they came to him. Journal your thoughts on these topics or write them as a prayer to God, whether you need to ask him questions about what you learned, thank him for what you learned, or ask him what to do next now that you have a better understanding. Also write down any observations or questions that you want to bring to your next group time.

NOTE
1. Craig S. Keener, *The IVP Bible Background Commentary: New Testament* (Downers Grove, IL: InterVarsity Press, 1993), p. 278.

SESSION SIX

VICTORIOUS SACRIFICE

Jesus said to her, "Your brother will rise again."
Martha answered, "I know he will rise again in the
resurrection at the last day." Jesus said to her, "I am the
resurrection and the life. The one who believes in me will live,
even though they die; and whoever lives by believing in me
will never die. Do you believe this?"

JOHN 11:23–26

OPENING REFLECTION

We envy childhood for its naivete and ease. But it doesn't take long—adolescence, or young adulthood perhaps—for us to start feeling the weight of life. Each year there is a new challenge . . . an unexpected illness . . . a new problem that causes us endless worry. The only thing harder than the trials of life is not knowing if or when they will end.

Enter Christ. Behold the empty tomb.

Jesus' ministry had come to an abrupt end on a cross. His followers had been devastated when they saw him arrested and heard the reports that he had been executed. Their dreams had been dashed. Their best friend and teacher was gone. What would they do now? What did this mean about Jesus' message they had helped spread—one of hope, healing, and freedom?

Mary Magdalene was one of those followers who was reeling from the events of the crucifixion. Her hope was gone. But then she saw him—the first of Jesus' followers to witness him alive. When she saw him, she "took hold of his feet, and worshiped him" (Matthew 28:9 NCV). In an instant, her life went from despair—she had lost Jesus—to hope as she saw he was back. The impossible was possible. The darkest night made way for the brightest day.

When Jesus defeated death, he dealt with our sin and provided us with unconditional forgiveness—but he also gave us the gift of hope. For if he could overcome death itself, what could he not help us to face? If he could be buried in darkness for three days and then emerge to life, what darkness of ours could he not dispel?

This is the beauty of our hardships while on earth. None of them *can* or *will* last forever. Because of Jesus, we can know—and believe—that even after the darkest of nights, joy comes with the morning.

TALK ABOUT IT

Begin your group time by inviting anyone to share his or her insights from last week's personal study. Next, to get things started, discuss one of the following questions:

- When was the first time you heard about the crucifixion and resurrection of Christ? How was the story explained to you?

  — *or* —

- What does it mean to you that Jesus was victorious over the grave?

VIDEO TEACHING NOTES

Play the video segment for session six. As you watch, use the following outline to record any thoughts or concepts that stand out to you.

NOTES

Perhaps you can relate to Mary's story. You've seen your hopes dashed. You wonder if Jesus sees you . . . and if he cares. The answer is a resounding yes! For "weeping may last through the night, but joy comes with the morning" (Psalm 30:5 NLT).

It had been an eventful few days. Earlier in the week, Jesus had entered the city riding on a donkey. He then brandish a whip and drive moneychangers from the temple. By mid-week, the hustling clerics were hatching a plot to kill him.

Jesus washed *all* the disciples' feet in the upper room—including Judas, whom he knew would betray him. But Jesus also knew he wouldn't be the only disciple to abandon him. Jesus said they would all turn away, fall away, and run away.

Jesus knows what it's like to smell the stench of Satan. He also knows what it's like to beg God to change his mind and to hear God say "no." For that is what God said to Jesus in the Garden of Gethsemane. And Jesus accepted the answer.

Even Peter turned his back on his friend and ran. He ended up following the torch-lit jury to the courtyard of Caiaphas. Three times people accused him of being with Jesus. Each time Peter denied. And each time Jesus heard his denial.

By nine o'clock, Jesus was stumbling to the cleft of Skull Hill, carrying a cross. The soldiers lifted it up when they reached it, placing Christ in the very position in which he came to die—between man and God. The sacrifice had been made.

Mary was there, witnessing the death of the one who had restored her to life. When Sunday arrived, she went to place warm oils on a cold body and bid farewell to the man who had given her reason to hope. But God was watching.

Jesus let Mary take hold of him. The other women, too, took hold of his feet and worshiped him. Jesus let them do so. Even if the gesture lasted for only a moment, he allowed it. The resurrected Lord was not too holy to be touched.

The resurrection reminds us that Jesus is the conquering King and the Good Shepherd. He has the power over death. But he also has a soft spot for the Mary Magdalenes of the world. For people like us. The regal hero is relentlessly tender.

GROUP DISCUSSION

Take a few minutes with your group members to discuss what you just watched and explore these concepts in Scripture.

1. Even if you've heard the crucifixion and resurrection story many times before, what new insights did you learn from today's teaching?

2. Read Matthew 26:31–35. According to this passage, how many of Jesus' disciples would fall away, or betray him, before his crucifixion?

3. How would you feel if you knew one of your best friends was going to betray you? What would you do? How would you treat this friend? What does it say about Jesus that he carried on with the crucifixion—an act that would benefit his disciples—even though he knew they would each walk away from him?

4. Read Matthew 26:36–46. When have you tried to avoid something painful that you knew was coming? What

does it say about Jesus that he asked God to change his
fate? What does it say about Jesus that he carried through
with God's plan?

5. Jesus' final words—"It is finished" (John 19:30)—was not
a cry of defeat but of victory. How did Jesus' death sym-
bolize victory? What does this victory mean for you today, in your everyday life?

6. Read John 20:11–18. How did Mary Magdalene react
when she realized that Jesus was alive? How did Jesus
respond to Mary?

7. Have you ever experienced resurrection in your own
life—a circumstance that went from hopeless to hopeful?
If so, what was the experience? What was it like for you?

8. What new insights do you have about the character of Christ based on today's study of the crucifixion, the events leading up to it, and the resurrection?

CLOSING ACTIVITY

Briefly review the outline for the video teaching and any notes you took. In the space below, write down which lesson from this study has meant the most to you: (1) God with Us, (2) Friend of Sinners, (3) Compassionate Physician, (4) Great Teacher, (5) Miracle Worker, or (6) Victorious Sacrifice. Once you are finished, go around the room and briefly discuss with the group why that particular lesson resonated with you and what you learned from it.

CLOSING PRAYER

Close your time together in prayer. You can either have one person lead the group in a final prayer, or you can read this prayer aloud: *"God, we thank you for sending your Son so we might know that you get us, see us, and understand us. Thank you for the sacrifice he made so we might know true forgiveness and seek righteousness in our lives. Help us encourage one another in the ways of Christ. May we see him at work around us, may we seek to be like him, and may others see him in us. In Jesus' name we pray, amen."* Record any prayer requests from your group members, and then commit to praying for those requests throughout the week. Also record any praise reports that people have to share.

NAME   PRAYER REQUEST / PRAISE REPORT

FINAL
PERSONAL
STUDY

Reflect on the material you have covered during your group time by engaging in the following activities. This week, you will engage with the passages that were covered during the teaching, looking at the different ways your life intersects with the story of the crucifixion and resurrection. Each personal study consists of three days of reflection activities to help you implement what you learned in the group time. The time you invest will be well spent, so let God use it to draw you closer to him. Be sure to share in the coming weeks with your group leader or group members any key points or insights that stood out to you.

PAIN

On the night before Jesus was crucified, he went into the Garden of Gethsemane and prayed that God would "take this cup" from him (Luke 22:42). The story reveals that Jesus understood the depth of the pain he would face on the cross, for at one point he was in such anguish that "his sweat was like drops of blood falling to the ground" (verse 44). As Matthew relates:

> ³⁶ *Then Jesus went with his disciples to a place called Gethsemane, and he said to them, "Sit here while I go over there and pray."* ³⁷ *He took Peter and the two sons of Zebedee along with him, and he began to be sorrowful and troubled.* ³⁸ *Then he said to them, "My soul is overwhelmed with sorrow to the point of death. Stay here and keep watch with me."*
> ³⁹ *Going a little farther, he fell with his face to the ground and prayed, "My Father, if it is possible, may this cup be taken from me. Yet not as I will, but as you will."*
> ⁴⁰ *Then he returned to his disciples and found them sleeping. "Couldn't you men keep watch with me for one hour?" he asked Peter.* ⁴¹ *"Watch and pray so that you will not fall into temptation. The spirit is willing, but the flesh is weak."*
> ⁴² *He went away a second time and prayed, "My Father, if it is not possible for this cup to be taken away unless I drink it, may your will be done"* (Matthew 26:36–42).

1. What did Jesus do before he entered into this time of considering what he would face the next day (see verse 36)?

2. Why do you think Jesus chose to take along Peter, James, and John with him (see verse 37)?

3. What did Jesus ask of God? What did he put above his own desires to avoid the pain of the cross that he knew was coming (see verses 39, 42)?

4. The cup that Jesus mentions may refer to the "cup of wrath" described several times in the Old Testament—a vessel for pouring out God's judgment on the nations (see Isaiah 51:17, 22; Jeremiah 25:15; Zechariah 12:2).[1] Jesus was about to suffer judgment and knew the punishment would be severe. When was a time in your life that you felt overwhelmed by sorrow, fear, anxiety, or a grief too difficult to bear? What was that experience like for you?

5. Have you ever wished for a different end to your story, a different fate, a different outcome for a particular circumstance? If so, what do you wish had gone differently?

6. Have you ever had a physical reaction to something heartbreaking or fear-inducing, or physical or emotional pain? If so, what were your thoughts at that moment?

7. What is your greatest pain today? The one that causes you to beg, "Take this cup from me"?

8. How does it feel to know Jesus understands this pain?

Closing reflection: There is something deeply human about Jesus' words and actions the night before his death. It's easy to miss these verses and focus on the events of the next day, but when we study this night in the Garden, we can't help but see our own experiences with pain, death, and sorrow. Jesus knew what it was like to beg God for anything else to happen. He knew what it was like to double over in sadness until his body could no longer hold him up and he fell to the ground, unable to do anything but cry to God for help, not knowing if God would. Jesus knew. Jesus knows. Today, whether you are feeling overwhelmed by something that's approaching or something that just happened, tell Jesus about it. Tell him about your pain, openly and honestly. Remember that he knows how you feel and can handle every detail.

BETRAYAL

Before Jesus was crucified, he was betrayed by those closest to him—his disciples. Peter denied him. Judas sold him out. The rest kept falling asleep when they were supposed to be keeping watch in the Garden of Gethsemane on the most difficult night of Jesus' life. Betrayal by a friend or loved one can cause some of our deepest pain. Today, you can find solidarity in Christ's experience with betrayal as you study the next part of the story:

> [43] *When he came back, he again found them sleeping, because their eyes were heavy.* [44] *So he left them and went away once more and prayed the third time, saying the same thing.*
>
> [45] *Then he returned to the disciples and said to them, "Are you still sleeping and resting? Look, the hour has come,*

and the Son of Man is delivered into the hands of sinners. ⁴⁶ *Rise! Let us go! Here comes my betrayer!"*

⁴⁷ *While he was still speaking, Judas, one of the Twelve, arrived. With him was a large crowd armed with swords and clubs, sent from the chief priests and the elders of the people.* ⁴⁸ *Now the betrayer had arranged a signal with them: "The one I kiss is the man; arrest him."* ⁴⁹ *Going at once to Jesus, Judas said, "Greetings, Rabbi!" and kissed him.*

⁵⁰ *Jesus replied, "Do what you came for, friend."*

Then the men stepped forward, seized Jesus and arrested him (Matthew 26:43–50).

1. Jesus asked his disciples twice to stay awake and keep watch with him as he prayed (see verses 38, 40–41). How do you think Jesus felt when he found them sleeping again for the third time (see verses 43–44)?

2. Have you ever been in a difficult situation and the friends you hoped would be there for you were not? What was the experience like for you? What is your relationship like with those friends or loved ones today?

3. Judas betrayed Jesus by turning him in to the authorities for money (see Luke 22:1–6.). What does Jesus' response

in this passage tell you about how Jesus felt about his betrayal (see verse 50)? Why do you think Jesus referred to Judas as *friend* in this verse?

4. Is there a "Judas" in your life today, or one from your past? Someone who betrayed or hurt you in the worst way? If so, what kind of feelings surface when you think about this person?

5. Matthew continues the story of Jesus' arrest and trial by depicting another disciple's betrayal:

[69] Now Peter was sitting out in the courtyard, and a servant girl came to him. "You also were with Jesus of Galilee," she said.

[70] But he denied it before them all. "I don't know what you're talking about," he said.

[71] Then he went out to the gateway, where another servant girl saw him and said to the people there, "This fellow was with Jesus of Nazareth."

[72] He denied it again, with an oath: "I don't know the man!"

^{73} *After a little while, those standing there went up to Peter and said, "Surely you are one of them; your accent gives you away."*

^{74} *Then he began to call down curses, and he swore to them, "I don't know the man!"*

Immediately a rooster crowed. ^{75} *Then Peter remembered the word Jesus had spoken: "Before the rooster crows, you will disown me three times." And he went outside and wept bitterly* (Matthew 26:69–75).

What did Peter claim about his relationship with Jesus? Why do you think he did this?

6. Have you ever had a friend or loved one talk poorly about you behind your back? If so, how did it feel when you found out what this person had said?

7. Jesus already knew that Peter was going to deny him (see Matthew 26:34). Yet he still shared a Passover meal with him and took Peter with him to the Garden of Gethsemane. Why do you think Jesus chose to do this? What does this tell you about his nature and character?

8. In these passages, how did Jesus respond to his betrayal in a human way? How did he respond in a divine way? What do you learn about how to handle betrayals from his example?

Closing reflection: It is not fun to think about the way you have been betrayed or those who have betrayed you. The pain cuts deep, and it is easier to just avoid revisiting it. But for the next few moments, bring any pain you have (or had in the past) from any betrayal to Jesus. Tell the Lord about that person. Tell him about that experience. Remember, he knows what this particular pain feels like. After you've shared this experience, be silent for a minute or two. What do you hear Christ telling you about your pain and the betrayal you've experienced? Use the space below to record what you hear or any thoughts that arise at this time.

RESURRECTION

Ultimately, the story of Jesus' crucifixion ends with the joy of resurrection. But it wasn't just Jesus who experienced resurrection. The followers of Christ—who just days before had believed their hopes had come to an end—experienced new life when they saw Jesus had conquered the grave. The story of Mary Magdalene meeting the risen Christ in particular reveals that resurrection is possible in each of our lives. John relates the first part of the story:

¹¹ *Now Mary stood outside the tomb crying. As she wept, she bent over to look into the tomb* ¹² *and saw two angels in white, seated where Jesus' body had been, one at the head and the other at the foot.*

¹³ *They asked her, "Woman, why are you crying?"*

"They have taken my Lord away," she said, "and I don't know where they have put him." ¹⁴ *At this, she turned around and saw Jesus standing there, but she did not realize that it was Jesus.*

¹⁵ *He asked her, "Woman, why are you crying? Who is it you are looking for?"*

Thinking he was the gardener, she said, "Sir, if you have carried him away, tell me where you have put him, and I will get him" (John 20:11–15).

1. What was Mary doing as this scene opens (see verse 11)?

2. Have you ever visited the gravesite of a loved one, much as Mary visited Jesus' tomb? What can you know about Mary and Jesus' relationship if she was one of the first to visit his grave?

3. Jesus spoke to Mary, but she didn't know that it was him (see verse 15). Why do you think she didn't recognize

Jesus? Why do you think Jesus didn't reveal his identity right away?

4. Now read the rest of Mary Magdalene and Jesus' story:

> *16 Jesus said to her, "Mary."*
> *She turned toward him and cried out in Aramaic, "Rabboni!" (which means "Teacher").*
> *17 Jesus said, "Do not hold on to me, for I have not yet ascended to the Father. Go instead to my brothers and tell them, 'I am ascending to my Father and your Father, to my God and your God.'"*
> *18 Mary Magdalene went to the disciples with the news: "I have seen the Lord!" And she told them that he had said these things to her* (John 20:16–18).

When did Mary recognize Jesus? How do you think Mary felt seeing Jesus alive at that moment?

5. Think of someone close to you who has passed away. How did you feel in the days following that person's death? What would you think or feel if you found out that loved one was alive?

6. Jesus is the only person in recorded history who had the power to bring about his own resurrection (see John 10:18). Yet we can experience resurrection in our lives as well. A relationship we thought was beyond repair is restored. A dream we thought would never come true becomes possible again. What is something that has been resurrected in your life? What is something you still want to see resurrected?

Closing reflection: As your time in this study comes to a close, think about Jesus' words to Martha: "I am the resurrection and the life. The one who believes in me will live, even though they die; and whoever lives by believing in me will never die. Do you believe this?" (John 11:25–26). Answer the question for yourself: *Do you believe this?* Spend some time before the man about whom you've been reading and learning. Ask Jesus your questions. Bring him your fears. Or simply sit in the joyful promise of your own resurrection.

NOTE
1. Craig S. Keener, *The IVP Bible Background Commentary: New Testament* (Downers Grove, IL: InterVarsity Press, 1993), p. 121.

LEADER'S GUIDE

Thank you for your willingness to lead a group through the *Jesus* small-group study by Max Lucado. What you have chosen to do is important, and much good fruit can come from studies like this. The rewards of being a leader are different from those of participating, and we hope that as you lead you will find your own walk with Jesus deepened by this experience.

The *Jesus* study is a six-session curriculum built around video content and small-group interaction. As the group leader, imagine yourself as the host of a dinner party. Your job is to take care of your guests by managing all the behind-the-scenes details so that as your guests arrive, they can focus on each other and on interaction around the topic.

As the group leader, your role is not to answer all the questions or reteach the content—the video, book, and study guide will do most of that work. Your job is to guide the experience and cultivate your small group into a kind of teaching community. This will make it a place for members to process, question, and reflect—not receive more instruction.

There are several elements in this leader's guide that will help you as you structure your study and reflection time, so follow along and take advantage of each one.

BEFORE YOU BEGIN

Before your first meeting, make sure the group members have a copy of this study guide so they can follow along and have their answers written out ahead of time. Alternately, you can hand out the study guides at your first meeting and give the group members some time to look over the material and ask any preliminary questions. During your first meeting, be sure to send a sheet of paper around the room and have the members write down their name, phone number, and email address so you can keep in touch with them during the week.

Generally, the ideal size for a group is between eight to ten people, which will ensure that everyone will have enough time to participate in discussions. If you have more people, you might want to break up the main group into smaller sub-groups. Encourage those who show up at the first meeting to commit to attending the duration of the study, as this will help the group members get to know each other, create stability for the group, and help you know how to prepare each week.

Each of the sessions begins with an opening reflection. The two questions that follow in the "Talk About It" section serve as an icebreaker to get the group members thinking about the topic at hand. Some people may want to tell a long story in response to one of these questions, but the goal is to keep the answers brief. Ideally, you want everyone in the group to get a chance to answer, so try to keep the responses to a minute or less. If you have talkative group members, say up front that everyone needs to limit the answer to one minute.

Give the group members a chance to answer, but tell them to feel free to pass if they wish. With the rest of the study, it's generally not a good idea to have everyone answer every question—a free-flowing discussion is more desirable. But with the opening icebreaker questions, you can go around the circle. Encourage shy people to share, but don't force them.

Before your first meeting, let the group members know that each session contains four between-sessions activities that they can complete during the week. While this is an optional exercise, it will help the members cement the concepts presented during the group study time and encourage them to spend time each day in God's Word. Also invite them to bring any questions and insights they uncovered while reading to your next meeting, especially if they had a breakthrough moment or didn't understand something.

WEEKLY PREPARATION

As the leader, there are a few things you should do to prepare for each meeting:

- *Read through the session.* This will help you to become familiar with the content and know how to structure the discussion times.

- *Decide which questions you definitely want to discuss.* Based on the amount and length of group discussion, you may not be able to get through all of the Bible study and group discussion questions, so choose four to five questions that you definitely want to cover.

- *Be familiar with the questions you want to discuss.* When the group meets you'll be watching the clock, so you want to make sure you are familiar with the questions you have selected. In this way, you'll ensure you have the material more deeply in your mind than your group members.

- *Pray for your group.* Pray for your group members throughout the week and ask God to lead them as they study his Word.

In many cases, there will be no one "right" answer to the question. Answers will vary, especially when the group members are being asked to share personal experiences.

STRUCTURING THE DISCUSSION TIME

You will need to determine with your group how long you want to meet each week so you can plan your time accordingly. Generally, most groups like to meet for either sixty minutes or ninety minutes, so you could use one of the following schedules:

SECTION	60 MIN.	90 MIN.
WELCOME (MEMBERS ARRIVE AND GET SETTLED)	5 min.	10 min.
ICEBREAKER (DISCUSS ONE OF THE TWO OPENING QUESTIONS FOR THE SESSION)	10 min.	10 min.
VIDEO (WATCH THE TEACHING MATERIAL TOGETHER AND TAKE NOTES)	20 min.	20 min.

SECTION	60 MIN.	90 MIN.
DISCUSSION (DISCUSS THE BIBLE STUDY QUESTIONS YOU SELECTED AHEAD OF TIME)	20 min.	40 min.
PRAYER/CLOSING (PRAY TOGETHER AS A GROUP AND DISMISS)	5 min.	10 min.

As the group leader, it is up to you to keep track of the time and keep things moving along according to your schedule. You might want to set a timer for each segment so both you and the group members know when your time is up. (Note there are some good phone apps for timers that play a gentle chime or other pleasant sound instead of a disruptive noise.)

Don't be concerned if the group members are quiet or if they are slow to share. People are often quiet when they are pulling together their ideas, and this might be a new experience for them. Just ask a question and let it hang in the air until someone shares. You can then say, "Thank you. What about others? What came to you when you watched that portion of the video?"

GROUP DYNAMICS

Leading a group through the *Jesus* study will prove to be highly rewarding both to you and your group members. However, this doesn't mean you will not encounter any challenges along the way! Discussions can get off track. Group members may not be sensitive to the needs and ideas of others. Some might worry they will be expected to talk about matters that make them feel awkward. Others may express comments that result in disagreements. To help ease this strain on you and the group, consider the following ground rules:

- When someone raises a question or comment that is off the main topic, suggest you deal with it another time, or, if you feel led to go in that direction, let the group know you will be spending some time discussing it.

- If someone asks a question you don't know how to answer, admit it and move on. At your discretion, feel free to invite group members to comment on questions that call for personal experience.

- If you find one or two people are dominating the discussion time, direct a few questions to others in the group. Outside the main group time, ask the more dominating members to help you draw out the quieter ones. Work to make them a part of the solution instead of the problem.

- When a disagreement occurs, encourage the group members to process the matter in love. Encourage those who are on opposite sides of the issue to restate what they heard the other side say about the matter, and then invite each side to evaluate if that perception is accurate. Lead the group in examining other Scriptures related to the topic and look for common ground.

When any of these issues arise, encourage your group members to follow these words from the Bible: "Love one another" (John 13:34), "If it is possible, as far as it depends on you, live at peace with everyone" (Romans 12:18), "Whatever things are true . . . noble . . . pure . . . lovely . . . if there is any virtue and if there is anything praiseworthy—meditate on these things" (Philippians 4:8 NKJV), and, "Be swift to hear, slow to speak, slow to wrath" (James 1:19 NKJV). This will make your group time more rewarding and beneficial for everyone who attends.

Thank you again for your willingness to lead your group. May God reward your efforts and dedication, equip you to guide your group in the weeks ahead, and make your time together in the *Jesus* study fruitful for his kingdom.

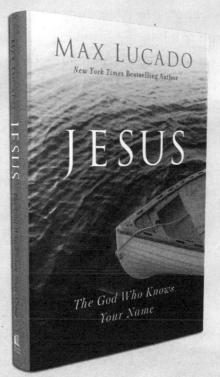

ALSO AVAILABLE
from MAX LUCADO

Unshakable Hope for All Ages

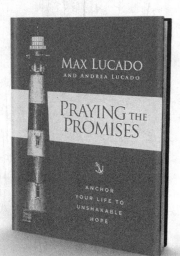

ADULTS

STUDENTS

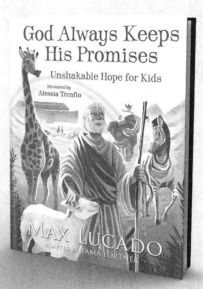

KIDS